UMBERTO FORTIS

the Ghetto on the lagoon

A GUIDE TO THE HISTORY AND ART OF THE VENETIAN GHETTO

(1516-1797)

REVISED EDITION
Translated by Roberto Matteoda

STORTI EDIZIONI

2

To the memory of my father and my mother
who loved the Venetian Ghetto
and taught me to love it too.

Front cover. Aerial photograph of the Ghetto Nuovo, Venice

(כז) וְהֵפִיץ יהוה אֶתְכֶם בָּעַמִּים,

וְנִשְׁאַרְתֶּם מְתֵי מִסְפָּר בַּגּוֹיִם,

אֲשֶׁר יְנַהֵג יהוה אֶתְכֶם שָׁמָּה.

(כט) וּבִקַּשְׁתֶּם מִשָּׁם אֶת יהוה אֱלֹהֶיךָ –

וּמָצָאתָ,

כִּי תִדְרְשֶׁנּוּ בְּכָל לְבָבְךָ וּבְכָל נַפְשֶׁךָ –

(ל) בַּצַּר לְךָ;

וּמְצָאוּךָ כֹּל הַדְּבָרִים הָאֵלֶּה בְּאַחֲרִית הַיָּמִים –

וְשַׁבְתָּ עַד יהוה אֱלֹהֶיךָ

וְשָׁמַעְתָּ בְּקֹלוֹ.

"And the Lord shall scatter you among the peoples,
and ye shall be left few in number among the nations,
whither the LORD shall lead you away...
But if from thence ye shall seek the LORD thy God,
thou shalt find him,
if thou search after him with all thy heart
and with all thy soul.
When thou art in tribulation,
and all these things are come upon thee,
in the latter days thou shalt return to the LORD thy God,
and hearken unto his voice."
(Deuteronomy IV, 27-30)

FOREWORD

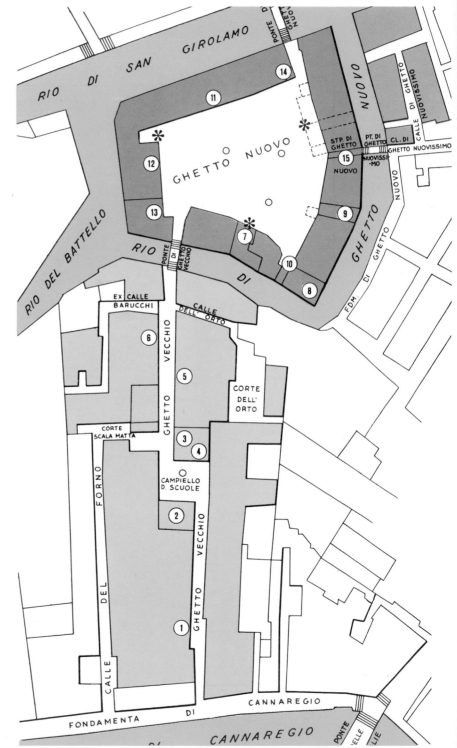

This guide to the Venetian Ghetto is new in its general approach and selection of details and can boast some originality in the matter of research, but does not claim to be exhaustive in its information. Restricted both by the scarcity of evidence and by limitations of space, but availing itself of the most reliable recent historical research, and concentrating mainly on the 16th and 17th centuries, it merely aims to pass on the latest scientific findings in popular form and, combining history with artistic and cultural factors, lead to a basic all-round view, from inside, of the rites, traditions, faith and civilization of this highly unusual and complex society.

The particular intention of this book exempts it from specific bibliographic and documentary references, and justifies its concern with architecture and town planning and its concentration on the descriptive element at the expense of historical analysis.

4

Map of the Venetian Ghetto

1 - The stone tablet in the Ghetto Vecchio
2 - Scola Spagnola
3 - Scola Levantina
4 - Scola Luzzatto (present site)
5 - Leon Modena Midrash
6 - Vivante Midrash
7 - Scola Italiana
8 - Scola Canton
9 - Scola Grande Tedesca - Museum of Hebrew Art
10 - The stone tablet in the Ghetto Nuovo
11 - Casa di Riposo Israelitica
12 - Holocaust Monument by Arbit Blatas
13 - Scola Mesullamim (original site)
14 - Scola Luzzatto (original site)
15 - Scola Kohanim (original site)
* - Sites of three pawnshops

Venice - Perspective map. Gio. Merlo 1696 (detail)

In the collective memory of the Jewish people the "ghetto" meaning not only a physical, urban entity but also a complex socio-cultural phenomenon, has always had an ambivalent significance. On the one hand, it has been perceived as the embodiment of forced segregation, discrimination against a minority by a society that presumes its own superiority and believes itself authorized to exclude from its own organization those regarded as "different" in culture, faith and traditions. This condition is materially endorsed by physical isolation, the presence of walls and gates, the humiliating state of subjection, the burden of oppressive taxation, the obligation to wear a distinguishing badge, and denial of the opportunity to benefit from common rights. On the other hand, from inside, it has been seen as the embodiment of an under-privileged people's heroic will to resist. They recognize the impossibility of a concrete reversal of their exclusion from the dominant society so, by dogged cultural commitment and stable religious belief, they have found a way to convert a disadvantageous condition imposed from outside into what in practice is a defensive structure, which has succeeded in preserving those very customs, rites and traditions that define an authentic Jewish identity, and defending it against the attraction of dispersive forces.

During almost three centuries of existence (1516-1797), the Jewish "seraglio" around San Girolamo in Venice was an exemplary reflection of this ambivalence. The system of the condotta *(ruling), the institution decreed by Venice in the confinement of "Judeans" the control that various official departments exercised over financial activity or sea trade, the continuous fiscal pressure, and the legal restrictions and prohibitions, all imposed from outside, were counterbalanced and almost compensated for from inside by the thorough depth of Talmudic studies and the interest in mystic interpretation of the Scriptures, the faith of the various ethnic groups — German, Italian, Levantine and Spanish — with the building of different synagogues, their re-*

5

spect for their own traditions in both language and folklore, their steady contribution towards the education of the young, the handing down of an independent and distinct culture in the collective consciousness in spite of internal friction and unrest, and the sense of belonging to a unique and "different" religious mould.

In addition to these common traits and the ethnic complexity of the groups living together, there is a third, perhaps less evident aspect that distinguishes the Ghetto on the Lagoon from any other ghetto in Italy, and that would be sought in vain in any other Italian community: the daily lives of the Venetian Jews over the years can be described as a constantly fluctuating relationship with the surrounding society, on both economic and cultural levels, which gives a unique character to the conflict between interior and exterior and to the very nature of the discrimination itself. Lying like a small city within a city but intimately involved with it, the Ghetto was guarded behind closed gates at night but by day the Venetian people would visit its pawnbrokers or rag-and-bone men, and Levantine merchants would go to the Rialto centre or have their wares carried to the port for shipment. Although it always remained a separate and autonomous world, its life regulated by different phases such as the liturgical deadline of the Sabbath and various solemn feasts, and with its own synagogues, schools and institutions, it was not unknown for Jewish scholars to take an interest in Venetian culture and for Venetian intellectuals to attend the sermons of a famous Rabbi. Recognizing their reciprocal value, the celebrated doctor Davide de' Pomis praised the "almost divine institutions" and the perfection of La Serenissima's orders, and Rabbi Simone Luzzato applauded the Venetian Republic's "stable and invariable form of Regiment" while on the other side the scholar and diarist Marin Sanuto recognized the need for the Jewish presence in Venice for the sake of the banks, and the Cinque Savi alla Mercanzia (today's Department of Trade) acknowledged the essential contribution made to the State economy by the great Levantine trade.

In all, although there were moments of tension, throughout centuries of coexistence the Venetian Ghetto constituted a fluent and complex phenomenon of combined exclusion and integration between the dominant society and the minority group, such as is unparalleled in the history of Italian Jewry. Certainly, the imposing buildings which can still be seen today, results of the clever adaptation of Venetian ideas to Jewish demands, the exceptional quality of Hebrew literature, an equally conspicuous result of the fusion of humanist interests and the contribution of the Jewish intelligentsia, and the collection of liturgical objects now appropriately displayed in a museum are together unequalled in any other community. Other ghettos have perhaps produced personalities of greater prestige, other seraglios have witnessed episodes that more obviously affected the history of the Diaspora of the Children of Israel, but not one has assumed such an absolutely specific character in its multiplicity of experience and its richness of cultural development as that which existed for centuries as the Università degli ebrei di Venezia (Università in the meaning of "Nation").

The true origin of Venice's Jewish community remains shrouded in the mists of time, in spite of remarkable recent historical research. It has long been known that the earliest dealings, commercial in nature, between the Jews and the Rialto centre date back at least to the 10th century. This is indirectly but conclusively confirmed by some documents which clearly betray suspicious reservations about Jewish activity. In 932, in fact, Doge Candiano II, harping on the traditional theme of Jewish "falsehood" exhorted Henry I of Germany to have all the Jews in his kingdom either converted or banished. A later provision of 960, which prohibited slave trading, forbade the acceptance of "Judeans" aboard Venetian ships, on express pain of financial penalty. Nevertheless, throughout the Republic's ascendancy in the Mediterranean, at least until the 14th century, it seems that temporary activity by Levantine merchants or German money-lenders was allowed, although permanent residence permits were never granted to Jews; the motive was probably the fear of possible Jewish competition rather than real religious prejudice. The most sensational discovery of recent historical research (Jacoby, Ashtor, Ravid, Zordan) seems to be the remarkable fact of a "city without Jews". A scrupulous reading of documentary sources has overturned the traditional firm belief that there was a conspicuous Jewish presence in Venice in the late Middle Ages (Ravà, Schiavi, Roth, Milano). All the proofs used to support the earlier hypothesis have, on checking, turned out to be baseless. It is a fact that a diploma of 1090 from Doge Vitale Falier speaks of a "Giudecca" meaning a Jewish quarter, but the text we have clearly refers to Constantinople, not to Venice. Similarly, the information as to the presence of 1300 "Hebrew" souls in Venice in 1152, published — with a historian's honest doubts — by Gallicciolli, proves to be unfounded; the date may be a copyist's error and should probably refer to a later era, perhaps 1555. Lastly, there is ample evidence that an edict of 1290, subjecting Jewish merchants to a tax of 5% on all imported and exported goods, refers to the Negroponte and has nothing to do with the Rialto. In the light of this recent view, even the perennial question about the Giudecca, the island lying in front of St Mark's, now acquires more considerable weight than before; according to tradition it housed a few Jewish families in the settlement on the Lagoon for some time after the year 1000. There appears to be no surviving documentation or any conclusive proof of this either, in any case not enough to justify certain theories that the derivation of the Venetian placename is somehow linked to Sephardic (Spanish) merchants or Ashkenazic (German) money-lenders. It seems unlikely that the island of Spinalunga, which in fact appears to assume the name *Giudecca* in contemporary texts, should have derived its name from having been a Jewish settlement — as happened, however, in other towns of the Diaspora, including Venetian colonies; unlikely too that it indicates any effective connection with Jewish society.

7

Venice, Museum of Hebrew Art: An 18th century *ḥanukkiyah*, 9-branched candlestick for the feast of *Ḥanukkah*, which celebrates the reconsecration of the Temple, desecrated in 165 B.C. by the Seleucids, and the victory of the Maccabees.

Venice, island of the Giudecca

On present indications, therefore, a view that was held canonical having been confuted, it seems necessary to await the second half of the 14th century before the story of the relationship between Venice and the Jewish nuclei shows any definite development. This happened as a consequence of precise economic and social conditions, which obliged *La Serenissima* to go back on its decisions and gradually revise its policies. Jews were excluded from the trade guilds, which meant they could not work as artisans, whereby they were often obliged to turn to moneylending for interest. The Venetian Republic could not undervalue this widening practice, nor the importance that the availability of their liquid capital, placed in circulation at a controllable interest rate, came to assume in the precapitalist structure of individual states' economies. Until 1254, in effect, Venice had opposed all activity concerning usury in the city, but had nevertheless allowed Jewish money-lenders to stay in the vicinity. By 1366 it had relaxed its attitude and concluded specific agreements with the *feneratores* (usurers) resident in Mestre. In 1382, in order to meet the urgently rising demand for liquid capital and heal the suffering economy weakened by the war against Chioggia, it allowed these money-lenders to carry on their business in the ancient city centre, officially for the first time, imposing interest rates fluctuating between 10% and 12%. Only

in this context, in 1385, with the agreement that fixed the terms of the relationship between the ruling power and the minority group, was the Senate's concession of the first *condotta* to Jewish money-lenders of German origin justified. This was an exceptional act in its way, admitting as it did a new ethnic group into the city and granting them *de facto* a well defined legal status. The conditions under which Simon, Jacob and Solomon of Nuremberg were received in the Rialto centre were certainly less than favourable, but that very compact, in the terms in which it was defined, contained the premises for the foundation of a stable Jewish colony on the Lagoon, and at the same time anticipated the guidelines for all future attitudes towards the community (Mueller). From then on, in fact, Jewish capital was always to be valued either in proportion to its availability in the credit sector, or as an inexhaustible source of compulsory loans to the State, while the permanent residence of the Jewish minority on the islands of the Lagoon was to be constantly assured in proportion to ever increasing tax pressure.

The new experiment, however, lasted only twelve years, under the control of the *Sopraconsoli*, amidst uncertainty and argument, between the desire to extend residence permits and strong pressure in the opposite direction. So it was that, whilst in 1386 the Jews were granted a stretch of land on San Nicolò di Lido for use as a cemetery, only eight

years later (1394), under the pretext of having discovered some irregularity in the conduct of a lending bank (but actually in the persistent fear of Jewish encroachment in various commercial spheres), the Senate decided that it would not renew the *feneratores' condotta* in 1397, but would expel them from the city, thereafter admitting them only for limited stays of two weeks at determined intervals, at the same time granting greater freedom of movement only to Jewish merchants from central and southern Italy. One phase had certainly ended, but already individual groups of Jews had established firm points of contact with the Lagoon area.

Venice - Correr Civic Museum: The Giudecca from the perspective map of the city of Venice (c.1500) attributed to J. de' Barbari, published by A. Kolb

Venice Lido

The ghetto as a compulsory residence for Jews behind an isolating wall originated in Venice in 1516, and during the second half of the same century it was imposed by the Church in many Italian cities. Nevertheless, even before its creation, throughout the centuries of their scattered existence, the Jews had always shown a tendency to live of their own free choice in quarters separate from the surrounding society, in order to keep their religious and cultural heritage alive, preserving it from contaminating forces, and be able to defend themselves better in the event of hostile demonstrations, under the shelter of the protection sometimes offered by the authorities. Such a quarter would be called the *giudecca* (or *judaica*, from

"Judaic"), and was a distinct sector of the town plan. There remain ample traces of them even today in the toponymy of many Italian towns, particularly in the south, and the whole Mediterranean basin in general, including Ferrara, Trani, Oria, and Costantinople, showing firm evidence of an ancient Jewish presence.

The fact that even in Venice the island of Spinalunga appears in late medieval documents denoted by the name of *Giudecca* has led historians of the 18th and 19th centuries to form a theory not only of a Jewish presence in Venice from the year 1000 onwards, but also of an effective connection, as in other towns of the Diaspora, between this presence and the etymology of the

name itself. On the basis of such theories, oral tradition, backed by Venetian scholars (Battaglia, Tassini and others) and Hebrew historians (Roth, Ottolenghi, Milano and others), has encouraged talk of the existence on the island of two synagogues supposed to have been demolished as late as the 18th century, also of the islanders' knowledge of the places which were presumed Jewish sites, and in conclusion of a stone engraved with Hebrew characters, found in the 19th century near the Zitelle, having come from the island itself. But in the Venetian case, checks carried out by more recent historians and the recognition that at least until the 14th century Venice admitted only passing trade with the Jews demand a radical review of the whole question. Not only can the existence of the Giudecca not be taken as proof of the settled presence of Jews in Venice before the late 14th century *condotta*, in these circumstances not even the origin of the island's name can confidently be connected with a Semitic pattern. Unless, in order to stay with tradition, one is prepared to believe that the name was used metaphorically ["like a Jewish quarter" (Cortelazzo-Zolli)], one must turn back to the hypothesis already considered by 18th century historians (Gallicciolli) of a possible connection of *Giudecca* with the Venetian *Zudegà* (of the judgement), referring to the *sentence* by which certain lands on the island of Spinalunga were supposedly assigned to some families of condemned conspirators by way of compensation. But the mystery of the Giudecca seems far from being solved and remains one of those tormented questions destined to give rise to endless learned disquisitions with no objective possibility of a solution.

9

One thing is certain, however: for a brief period in the late 14th century, the principal way for a limited number of Jews to gain entry to the ancient town centre of Venice — and other cities — was by the practice of pawnbroking. Between the 13th and 14th centuries, this phenomenon radically altered the role and conditions of Jews in Italian society. Several Italian towns used Jewish capital to advantage, under strict control, to meet the needs of the population's poorer classes, and it was when Venice also realized the possibilities of this practice that money-lenders from Mestre obtained their first *condotta*, which admitted them to the Rialto centre.

The spread of Jewish usury had really occurred in the late Middle Ages, affected by the different positions assumed by Judaism and Christianity towards the morality of moneylending for interest, and also as a consequence of the particular socio-economic situation in which the Jews found themselves after their exclusion from trade guilds that had a religious character. In fact the Old Testament says that loans to members of the same religion are to be regarded merely as acts of solidarity, and interest should be charged only to outsiders and in exceptional cases, whereas medieval rabbinical literature, under the impact of certain social changes and in spite of the opposition contained in the *Talmudh*, comes to the conclusion that every loan is a commercial transaction and therefore endorses the request for interest. The Church, adopting Aristotle's principle that coinage cannot earn coinage, and applying the evangelical exhortation *mutuum date*, *nihil inde sperantes*, had always forbidden usury, inserting its prohibition in the *Corpus Juris Canonici* with the famous *usura est usus pretium*. But since this intransigence caused great hardship, particularly among the poorest people, it was often disre-garded in daily practice, and money-lending was sometimes practised at exhorbitant rates of interest and with continual recourse to strategies designed to present a prohibited action in a favourable light. The Lateran Council of 1215 only forbade Jews to collect ''grave and immoderate sums'' thereby in fact sanctioning Jewish moneylending. Subsequently the Church's threats towards its own followers became harsher, while the birth of trade guilds of a religious nature excluded the Jews from any other possible activity. Furthermore, the Jews were forbidden any investment in fixed assets, so the only path open for their liquid capital was the usury market, and the possibility of control on the part of the authorities, by imposing limited interest rates, indirectly forced them into a precise role in society.

The anti-Jewish campaign launched in the 15th century by the Grey Friars with the setting up of the ''Monti di Pietà''lending banks offering interest-free or low-interest loans was not much of an obstacle to them, not even when the banks lost their early philanthropic nature and became small credit institutions. As a result, the practice of Jewish usury assumed a social role of primary importance, particularly in Venice where the Monti di Pietà banks were never admitted, and it was always to be an essential guarantee for the Jews that their city residence permits would be renewed, until the end of the 16th century, when it developed into a real sacrifice for the Venetian community.

After the establishment of a community in any city, one of the first official acts was always to request the authorities for concessions such as to guarantee the free performance of religious functions and the carrying out of spe-

10

London - British Museum: The allegory of usury (14th C.) (Ms. Add. 26795 f. 7v)

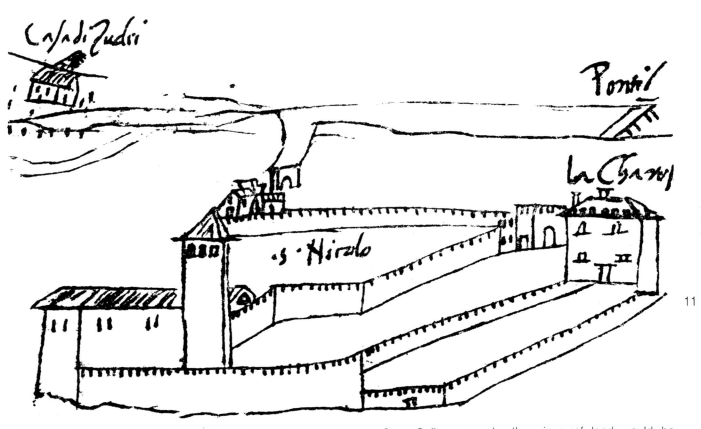

Casa di Zudei

Pontil

La Chiesa

s. Hirolo

cial rites and ceremonies. The need to build a synagogue was less urgent, as prayers can easily be said in private oratories provided the minimum required number of ten men are present (*minyan*), but individual groups always gave high priority to securing a piece of land for use as a cemetery. There was no choice in this matter because of the difference in funeral customs compared with Christian ones, and the need to avoid displays of hostility against the various expressions of mourning. And so it happened at Venice. "Deluding themselves that their residence could be endless" comments Gallicciolli, "the Jews turned their minds to the acquisition of a plot that might serve for the interment of their corpses." In fact, besides asking for ritual, cultural and educational concessions, an early sequel to the 1385 *condotta* was a request from the Jews for a space for the burial of their dead. On 25 September 1386, the Piovego magistrate therefore grant-

ed to Solomon, resident at Santa Sofia, and to Crisante, resident at Sant'Apollinare, representing the whole Jewish group, a tract of land measuring 70 by 30 paces, in a desolate, uncultivated place on the Lido, near the Benedictine monastery of San Nicolò. Protected, or intended to be, from any outrage or profane act, thus was born the ancient Jewish cemetery of Venice, which was to receive the mortal remains of Jews from the Lagoon community for more than four centuries.

For some time the Benedictine monks continued to lay claim to the land granted to the Jews, but in February 1389 the long controversy was settled (After the founding of the Ghetto, since Jews could not possess fixed

assets, the piece of land would be offered to the community on perpetual lease for use as a cemetery; a twenty-nine-year contract stipulated that an annual rent would be paid at Michaelmas; a warden's house would be prescribed, the site of which is shown on the documents as "Casa di Zudei"). Only a month before the original agreement, on another request from the Jews, the Piovego magistrate had allowed certain Simon and Moses to wall the cemetery, "propter enormia quae fiebant ad corpora Judeorum" in other words, because of the continual profanation of the tombs.

A monument with an obelisk is still standing today, its double inscription in Hebrew and Italian recording the inauguration of the hallowed ground in 1389. From that date, the wall underwent many extensions and some displacement, fulfilling its role almost uninterruptedly until the gates of the Ghetto were removed. It was not until the

French invasion that the surrounding walls were knocked down and creeping decay attacked the assembled monuments.

Venice, Lido - Ancient Jewish Cemetery: Monument with obelisk

Venice, Lido - Ancient Jewish Cemetery: Tombstone of Shemu'el b. Shimshon, d. 5150 (1389)

Naked and desolate / Is that ground; and scattered about / With solitary stones . . . (G. Prati, *Edmenegarda*, lines 64-66). In the early 19th century, the fascination of the abandoned cemetery's ruined solitude drew a romantic response from poets such as Goethe, Byron, Shelley and George Sand. But it was not truly rediscovered until later in the century. In 1881 Berliner, using a manuscript by M. Soave, published the texts of two hundred inscriptions. In 1884, when the Campo di Tiro a Segno (Shooting Range) was built, excavations brought old graves to light, and more tombstones surfaced during further work in 1925 and 1929. Thus began the recovery of an impressive heritage, not only from the artistic point of view, for the admirable craftsmanship of much funeral masonry and the literary value of many inscriptions, but also from the documentary point of view, for the considerable contribution to the study of Venetian-Jewish names and the crests of the most distinguished families in the Ghetto. Of the gravestones recovered, the most ancient is that of one *Shemu'el b. Shimshon*, who died in 5150 (1389), the very year that the cemetery was established. With such important finds available, relating to some of the most prestigious figures in the history of the Venetian Jews, the work of Pacifici (1929) and Bernstein (1935), alongside Ottolenghi and Sullam, initiated a phase of collection and study of epigraphic and iconographic material that has been completed in recent years by Boccato, Canarutto, Hertzberg, Luzzatto and Mortara, and has become crucial to our knowledge of the history of Venetian Jewry.

12

Throughout the 15th century, the chance to stay in the Rialto centre, even briefly, enabled increasingly numerous groups of Jews to settle in Venice (Ashtor, Jacoby). Although, in 1409, Venice stipulated that four months had to elapse between Jewish bankers' stays in the city, and in 1426 forbade them to have synagogues, the San Canciano and San Giuliano quarters were infiltrated by German merchants from mainland Veneto, where the *condotte* ensured a fairly tranquil existence, commercial operators from central and southern Italy, active in the mercantile-marine sector, scholars and men of culture, besides doctors, who had always been welcome in the old city centre. The Jewish presence, amply documented in decrees and legal pleadings, clearly aroused conflicting sentiments. Venice's official attitude was ever divided between political opportunism, inclined to accept the Jewish minority in gratitude for its economic contribution, and religious zeal, which thrust in the opposite direction. It was also affected on one side by violently anti-Jewish pressure from the Grey Friars, and on the other by open-

Venice - Correr Civic Museum: Map of Venice and Mestre by B. Bordone (1547)

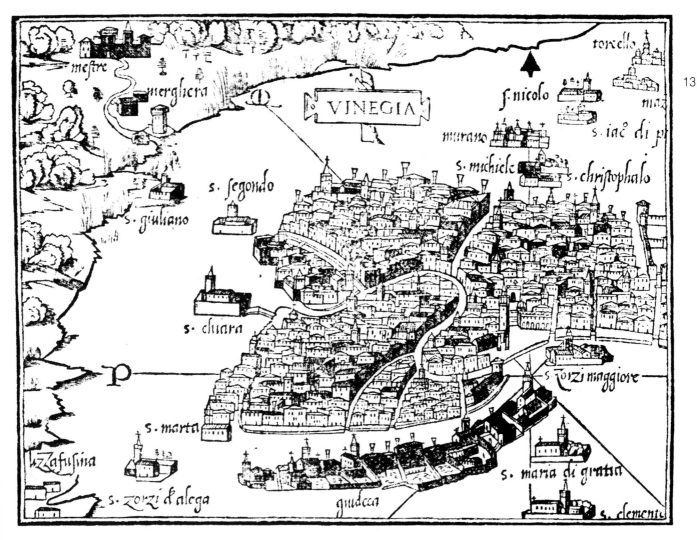

mindedness towards Jewish culture encouraged by the more serious intellectuals. The religious hostility was fanned by the Franciscans' heated campaign against usury, in which they accused the Jews of causing public poverty, at the same time seeking to maintain their own Monti di Pietà banks in competition with Jewish credit, all of which created inevitable tension and friction. On the other hand, interest in Jewish culture and language was fostered by many humanists who, although ideologically hostile to the *Talmudh*, were strongly attracted in their studies by the fascination of certain propositions derived from Cabalistic mysticism. Venice jealously guarded its right to make independent decisions, but was equally anxious to base those decisions on authoritative opinion, so in 1463 the Papal Legate, Cardinal Bessarion, was consulted about the advisability of allowing Jews into the city. The Cardinal replied in favour of accepting them, but always respecting the limitations imposed by the 14th century *condotta*. The following year Venice — ever hostile to the Monti di Pietà banks — granted the Jews a certain freedom on the cultural level and recognized them as Venetian citizens legitimately intent on the constant improvement of their status (Ashtor). By comparison with the hardships undergone in other lands of the Diaspora, particularly the repressive measures of the Spanish Inquisition, culminating in expulsion from Spain in 1492 and from Portugal in 1497, Venice's attitude would up to a point appear exceptionally cooperative, and the Jews themselves did not fail to appreciate this, praising Venice not only as a hospitable place but also as an outstanding example of constitutional stability and social harmony.

Nevertheless, towards the end of the century this harmony was disturbed by movements of dramatic unrest, besides traditional restrictions; in 1480 the rulers were powerless to oppose a death sentence passed on three Jews accused of ritual murder in a case at Porto Buffolè; five years later they managed to avoid tragic results from similar events at Marostica, but in 1496 they

failed to reject a proposal to reduce the money-lenders' residence permits to one a year. This in practice meant once more banishing Jewish groups from the old city centre to Mestre or other mainland towns, where a few surviving place-names such as *Piraghetto* in Mestre, the *Ghetto* district in Mogliano, *Via Giudecca* in Mirano, or *Via Ghetto* in Chirignago are indications of a former Jewish presence. But these were all marginal events, or limited to those who, like the Spanish Jews, chose to leave their homes rather than accept an enforced conversion. Venice's renown, already widespread in the 14th and 15th centuries, grew into a legend in the fertile ground of Jewish intellectual minds.

Mantua - S. Andrea: Dedication of S. Maria della Vittoria (detail), The banker Norsa wearing the Jewish badge

The truth was that there were many burdens and restrictions weighing on the Jews, in effect the sign of a discriminatory attitude.

Besides the more or less compulsory choice of moneylending or the small usury market, Jews were in fact confined to a limited number of occupations, most of which came under the "rag-and-bone" label, buying and selling used garments and related activities; they could not own land or other fixed assets; they were sometimes forced to attend Christian services or submit to baptism; they were often accused of most hideous crimes such as ritual murder, the profanation of the Host, or the poisoning of wells. But the most humiliating and lasting expression of hostility towards them was undoubtedly the imposition of a badge (the *siman*) to distinguish them from other people. This was decreed by Pope Innocent III during the Lateran Council of 1215, and applied to persons over the age of

thirteen, ostensibly to avoid any possible sexual promiscuity, but undoubtedly suggested for discriminatory reasons. Over the years the badge took different forms. At first it was a yellow circle stitched on the left shoulder of jackets or cloaks for men, and a yellow scarf for women; at the end of the 15th century this became a yellow beret and, later, a red one; sometimes exemption was granted to doctors, bankers (1502), and certain Levantines, also to students at Padua University, who were obliged to wear a black cap instead.

The violent accusations hurled against the Jews by the Grey Friars achieved their most tragic consequences in the Veneto region when Bernardino of Siena, John of Capistrano and Bernardino of Feltre preached that the "most perfidious Jews" were primarily responsible for the sufferings of society, accused them of the most heinous crimes, and succeeded in arousing waves of antisemitic hatred, particularly during Easter Week. The most famous and sensational case of this sort happened in Trent in 1475, when Brother Bernardino of Feltre delivered a violent sermon in which he accused the Jewish community of murdering a boy called Simon, and they were all driven out of the city. The boy later became the Blessed Simonino. Even Venice, which had always restrained violence and unjust accusations, was unable on one occasion to avoid the sacrifice of three innocent men.

Just before Easter 1480, the body of a child, Sebastiano Novello, was found at Porto Buffolè, in the Treviso region, and the Jewish community was accused of ritual murder. On 5 July, Servadio

from Porto Buffolè, Moses son of David from Treviso and Jacob son of Simon from Cologne, "most impious and most perfidious Judeans" were condemned to death by the Senate of the Venetian Republic, while other accused men were given lighter sentences. On 6 July, the three were taken along the Grand Canal on a barge to be exposed to public mockery, then had to walk back to St Mark's, where they were burned on specially erected stages between the two columns on the Piazza (Radzik).

There is a traditional belief, recorded by Sabbadini and repeated by Ottolenghi, that there is a connection between this episode and an inscription that stands today in the *Ghetto Nuovo* (New Ghetto), at the corner of the square, by the entrance to the Scola Canton. It bears a verse from *Psalms* (XXXII, 10): "*Rabbim makh'obhi(m) larasha' weḥaboṭeaḥ ba ('Adhonay) hesedh yesobhebhennu* — Many sorrows shall be to the wicked, but he that trusteth in the Lord, mercy shall compass him about". It is supposed to have been engraved, in memory of his last conversation with one of the accused, by one Joseph, the *ḥazzan* (officiant) of Porto Buffolè, who had come to Venice to support his fellow Jews in their last moments on earth. Evidently, one of the condemned men spotted him among the crowd and, referring to his accuser, recited the first line of the verse, and he, clearly intending to console him, reminded him of the second line. But there is no record of how the tablet came to be in Venice.

15

Venice - Campo di Ghetto Nuovo: Stone tablet beside the entrance to the Scola Canton

During the latter half of the 15th century the aversion felt towards the Jews was to some extent counterbalanced by a humanistic interest in their culture, which was manifest in Venice, among other places. Scholars and doctors of great renown such as Elia del Medigo, 'Abhraham de Balmes and Elia Levita were sought out by intellectuals like Pico della Mirandola or Cardinal Grimani, anxious to learn the sacred language wherewith to gain access directly to the Bible text and the most important Cabalistic sources; they created a close network of relationships between two peoples still worlds apart. Even the printing sector, still in its first decade, was inevitably influenced by the new atmosphere. Aldo Manuzio (1449-1515) in Venice, the first Italian printer, was also the first to use Hebrew characters in his publications, including works by Poliziano and Colonna, a Hebrew grammar for beginners, and a sample page for a planned edition of the Bible in three languages. This flourish of printing in Hebrew was the start of one of the most striking phenomena of 15th century Venetian culture, and it demonstrated something else, that is, a new open-mindedness towards the Jews, which, though sharply limited by fully sanctioned restrictions, was quite remarkable when measured against the persecutions they were undergoing elsewhere, in the Iberian peninsula and Central Europe.

16

It therefore seems reasonable, in such a climate, that a Spanish refugee arriving in Venice in 1503, obliged by the threat of forced conversion or persecution to leave his home and the prestige he enjoyed, should have sung the praises of the Venetian Republic's constitution, thus making his own contribution to the legend that was building up over that period. Don Yitzḥaq Abrabanel, a person highly esteemed in the field of Jewish culture and a top-ranking politician, landed at the Lagoon when Venice was at the summit of her powers and the repercussions of the early 15th century crisis had not yet been felt. Compared with the experiences he had been through, Venice

seemed to him such an example of stability and social harmony that, applying a typically medieval mode of comparison, and taking Mosaic law as a point of reference, he saw it as the realization of a perfect republican institution.

For some time historians and chroniclers had been helping to build up this legend, basing it on certain fundamentals: the sovereign and independent birth of the Republic, the unanimous conviction of the State's integrity and autonomy, the absence of internal strife — very different from the factions that undermined other city states — and the harmony and perfection of the constitution, guaranteed by the perfect co-operation between the various authorities. And Don Yitzḥaq could do no better than associate himself with these principles in his *Commentary* on the *Torah*, quoting the Bible in support. Having expressed his absolute pref-

erence for the republican regime, he thought he saw reflections in the structure of the Venetian Republic, the *Pregadi* (Special Councillors), the *Consiglio dei Dieci*, and the *Maggior Consiglio* of the three categories of rulers laid down in Mosaic law, a perfect composition able to guarantee stable government, justice, and co-operation between the various social classes.

Certainly, his feeling of deference and gratitude to the country that had sheltered him finally swamped any objective evaluation of the political reality that was, in fact, ambivalent, and would, within a short time, take shape in the creation of the Ghetto. But it is significant that, in spite of the restrictions and impositions in force in Veneto, even the Jews should have felt the urge to praise the Venetian State, which was in any case preferable in its pragmatic way to the terrible conditions under which they were forced to live elsewhere.

THE GHETTO NUOVO

The establishment of the Ghetto in the early 16th century was motivated by precise economic and fiscal considerations not unconnected with the persistent pressures of religious prejudice, so, although it does constitute a landmark in the history of the Jewish Diaspora, it cannot appear unexpected or revolutionary. On the contrary, it was clearly a compromise solution, the final outcome of the strategy towards the Jews already pursued by Venice for centuries. Always torn between the instinct to exclude foreign ethnic groups and a rational opportunistic readiness to accept them, *La Serenissima*'s attitude seems to have crystallized into the steady admission of a Jewish minority into the city, conditional upon their physical and moral segregation from the rest of society and the tiresome control of a notoriously severe magistrature.

It was therefore a point of arrival for the Jews, and passing from the restless life of continual migration in single families to the static condition of compulsory confinement in an entire group meant a radical change in their social, cultural and religious way of life.

On the positive side, such a solution does seem to be the necessary condition for the birth of a true community. Its implementation can be identified in the clauses of the *condotta* renewed in 1509 for the money-lenders from Mestre, which provided for the possibility of transferring the bankers themselves and their goods into the city in case of danger (Mueller). Six years later in fact, in 1509, following the defeat of Venice by troops of the Cambrai League at Agnadello, the violent pillage carried out by the imperial militia in the Veneto territory prompted many Jews to take refuge in the old city centre, scattered mainly in the San Cassiano, Sant'Agostino, San Geremia and San Polo districts.

Their presence was increasing day by day, and was made more disturbing by the inevitable difficulty of living alongside the local population and the consequent invectives of the Grey Friars, Brother Ruffino Lovato in particular. There is no doubt that this would have provoked the umpteenth expulsion two years later, in 1511, already decreed, in fact, by the *Avogadori de Comun*, had not an inter-departmental controversy with the *Consiglio dei Dieci* caused the drastic decision to be withdrawn. The Jewish community had by now closed its ranks and found in the person of Anselmo del Banco a valiant representative and defender against the State. Anselmo was a very powerful banker of great prestige; he had been

17

imprisoned, but released on payment of 10.000 ducats; he always managed to persuade *La Serenissima* of the value of the Jewish economic contribution during times of recession as a conclusive argument for the admission of Jews into the city, and always resisted the State's most unfavourable decisions. So he did when, in 1515, permission was given to open new shops on the Rialto, suggesting a more relaxed attitude towards the Jewish minority, and this rekindled old resentments in religious quarters, particularly in the sermons of Brother Giovan Maria d'Arezzo; this prompted the decisive intervention of Zorzi Emo in the College, with his proposal to confine all Jews on the Giudecca. Anselmo del Banco opposed the project, stressing the dangers inherent in the presence on the island of mercenary troops, and suggesting the preferable alternative of a settlement on Murano. His efforts, however, were in vain. The Senate was not long reaching a decision, and in March 1516 accepted the proposal of the scholar Zaccaria Dolfin to confine all Jews living in the city and all subsequent arrivals to the Ghetto island around San Girolamo, having built surrounding walls and drawbridges, imposed strict supervision by guards along the canal, and stationed porters at the gates, which were to be shut one hour after sunset in summer and two hours after sunset in winter and not opened until dawn. The Venetian powers had thus arrived at their predictable solution; discussions in fact continued for several years as to the desirability of having Jews in Venice at all, but doubt was never cast on the policy of keeping them segregated in a separate district, clearly divided from the rest of the population. The world's first *ghetto* had been created.

In three days from 29 March 1516, the Senate "Party" escorted about seven hundred Jews, Germans and some Italians, into the existing houses in the Ghetto Nuovo round San Girolamo, a "very capacious place". The "plot of land . . . called the *getto* or *ghetto* . . . was the site of the public foundry, where

mortars were cast, and of its official governor. The foundry had been there since the XIVth century . . . but had ceased to exist in the early XVth."

So writes Tassini in his *Curiosità Veneziane*, based on 14th and 15th century documents, including the testimony of Sabellico. It here transpires that the place "*vocabatur el getto quia erant ibi ultra duodecim fornaces et ibi fundebatur aes* - was called *el getto* because there were over twelve furnaces and bronze was cast there". The Italian *getto* means "casting" and the Venetian *geto* means "foundry". Nowadays this etymology still seems to be the one which invites most credence from scholars (Stern, Berliner, Teza, Cassuto, Spitzer, Toaff, Ravid, Marin and others), while other less sound though amply documented theories are not abandoned. Some, in fact, have linked the term with the Talmudic *get*, meaning "reject card" referring to the rejection of the Jews by the rest of

society (Sanders, Giacomelli, Philipson etc), others with the German *gehegt*, meaning "enclosed" (Hoffe, Beranek, etc), others with the old French *gueat*, meaning "guard" referring to the imposed supervisors (Wolf), others still with the Genoese *getto*, meaning "jetty, quay" where in 1492 the Jewish refugees from the Iberian peninsula were supposed to have been "cast" (Sermoneta); others have unearthed testimony in Yiddish earlier than the 16th century (Shmeruk), and still others have thought of the German *Gitter* ("grille"), the Italian *borghetto* ("district"), or the old English *gatwon* ("street") (Roth, etc) but these are all barely reliable assumptions. The only certainty is that Venice not only wins the dubious prize for being the first to confine the Jews in an isolated enclosure, but enjoys the etymological distinction of having coined a term now used all over the world.

"Est is undique ut insula circumfluus; recentiorem jactum nominant" runs Sabellico's description of 1490 - "the area is surrounded by water on all sides like an island; they call it the Ghetto Nuovo." Where the parishes of San Geremia and Santi Ermagora and Fortunato (Santa Marcuola) meet, now San Alvise, near San Girolamo, the Ghetto Nuovo first appeared, at the time the Jews were confined, as an open space completely surrounded by two-storey buildings and cut off all round by canals (Rio di San Girolamo, Rio della Masena, Rio degli Agudi, later Rio di Ghetto Nuovo, Sacca and Rio delle Monache, later Rio del Battello). There were only two exits, probably with drawbridges, one towards the San Girolamo embankment (Ponte di San Girolamo, later Ponte di Ghetto Nuovo), the other towards the Ghetto Vecchio (Old Ghetto), (Ponte degli Agudi, later Ponte di Ghetto Vecchio). It was a perfect, almost natural isolation, although in the middle of a city, unequalled by any subsequent enclosure in Italy. In fact, after 1555, when Paul IV's papal bull *Cum nimis absurdum* imposed "the Hebrew seraglio" in Rome and in the Papal State, every Italian city except Leghorn sooner or later set up its own ghetto with walls and gates, but none ever offered that sense of absolute physical isolation generated in the Venetian one, though sometimes they looked even more miserable and depressing inside. In spite of this, no other segregated community found a way of living in flexible and open rapport with the surrounding society, as they did in Venice.

19

The settlement of Jews in an outlying area of the city, well away from the main thoroughfares, caused a radical change in the ways of life of the various ethnic groups and in the structure of their host itself.

In a sense, after the inevitable initial friction arising from never having experienced such cohabitation, the establishment of different groups in one place encouraged the gradual formation of a community spirit that transcended individuals, expressing itself in the setting up of a representative body for dealings with the State, the formation of organizations and institutions able to meet the various demands of Jewish life, and the development of cultural forms in many respects unprecedented. Therefore the island of separation and segregation became totally transformed even in its rhythms of daily life. In contrast with the surrounding city, with which it nevertheless had a guaranteed flexible rapport, its new circumstances led to the development of a typically Jewish rhythm of life, a rhythm of worship governed by the regularity of the three daily prayers and the morning reading, the dates of high feasts or days of atonement, all revolving about the kingpin of the Sabbath, the real element connoting the Jewish world, so moving towards the slow consolidation of a pattern of rituals and traditions, habits and memories, destined to become the characteristic spiritual heritage of modern Jewry.

In another way, however, the very building of synagogues and schools, *yeshibhoth* and *midhrashim* (rabbinical schools and seminaries) alongside pawnbrokers first, then workshops, led to the complete transformation of the Ghetto area from the featureless space of the Venetian "corte" (courtyard) into a real "campo" (square) organized in Jewish style around certain characteristic poles, typical of the "new" life imposed by *La Serenissima* on the guest minority (Carletto). Very soon the existing houses, under the pressures of overpopulation, began to grow in height and undergo an internal transformation according to precise conventions of partitioning while, as a sign of their newly achieved stability, the new tenants established ties with the Christian proprietors on the basis of the institution of a *yus gazagà* (Hebrew *ḥazaqah* - possession), the right to perpetual residence, which could even be handed down, drawn up specifically to contain the rent levels and avoid too startling price rises.

In short, the changes and innovations actually led to the building up of that unique and inimitable microcosm that the Jews themselves, in their typical Jewish-Venetian parlance, developed over the years from German and Iberian expressions mixed with Venetian dialect, referred to as *hasèr*, the enclosed and isolated space that the Jewish spirit brought to life in a singular way.

In the distorted image created by anti-semitic prejudice there existed a persistent suspicion about the well-poisoning Jew, which made people contemplate with fear the prospect of Jews using public water-sources. This, alongside the confinement of a conspicuous group of people in a restricted space, may explain the presence in the Ghetto Nuovo of three well-heads intended for the exclusive use of the inhabitants. The ancient style, certainly prior to the 16th century, and the form of the decorative escutcheons on the sides, likewise possibly dating from the 15th century, do not seem fully attributable to conservationist ideals, as some would have it, on the part of the makers. It seems more likely that they were a ritual adaptation to the needs of the immigrant minority of materials already present, dating from the 15th century. The almond shaped escutcheons of the oldest well-head (by the present *Casa di Riposo*)

and the gothic ones of the other two seem to have been rubbed down in order to carve the three lions of Judah on all three, following the custom of the Ghetto (Rizzi). Not one of the wells, the first in Istrian stone, the others in pink marble from Verona, with their cylindrical barrels and simple decoration of shields and rosettes, can claim particular artistic distinction, nor does their form appear to recall — as a long tradition maintains — the arms of some 16th century superintendent.

◀ Venice - Campo di Ghetto Nuovo

Venice - Campo di Ghetto Nuovo: 15th century well-head

During the early years of compulsory residence there slowly developed the outlines of a status that would always govern the lives of the Ashkenazi "nation". The "Germans" under the control of the Cattaver officials provided Venice with a constant financial reserve; when an intense debate as to whether or not to renew their *condotta* came up in the Senate, the pragmatic evaluation of men like Sanuto and Grimani proved them a necessary presence, in this sense, for the State economy. The former maintained that they were as essential as bakers, and it would have been a serious mistake to drive them away, since there was no Monti di Pietà alternative in the city. "The Hebrews are necessary to subsidize the poor people" confirmed the latter. "No matter whether they live in the ghetto or go to live in Mestre" as long as it were allowed for "the Jews to practise usury". In a way, therefore, they were forced to run the Ghetto pawn shops through their own bankers, and pay a heavy annual tribute (including 10.000 ducats for the Arsenal), the responsibility for collecting which fell on the community's administrative body. The only other choice of work allowed them was the rag-and-bone trade, except for the privileged few who practised medicine or were employed in the printing of Hebrew books. They were truly difficult years, also because they lived under the constant threat of expulsion, sought mainly by a wide patrician fringe and constantly invoked by the vehement preaching of the Grey Friars. The laws concerning banking show, in fact, how detailed the regulations were, and how strict the control imposed by the magistrature, who always pursued the double aim of offering sound support to Venice's poorer people and preventing individual operators from making too high a profit. The rate of interest was originally fixed at 15-20%, but very soon, dropped, causing great losses and continual deficit (Poliakov, Pullan). Yet those very debts, heavy as they were, formed a permanent anchor and lifebelt for the Ghetto Nuovo residents.

The Monti di Pietà bank had often demonstrated itself barely efficient. It

21

had, moreover, lost sight of its early humanitarian function, and in 1523-4 the idea of opening a branch in Venice was finally thrown out. After that, the influx of Jewish money in the borrowing sector became so crucial, especially under the difficult economic conditions of 1527, that in 1528 the decree of expulsion issued the previous year under pressure from the anti-Semitic faction, notably from the sage Gabriele Moro, was revoked (Jacoby), and the value of the Jewish presence positively confirmed.

Nevertheless, the following decade — at least until 1537 — was marked by a continuous stream of proposals to exclude the Jews from the city, or to impose increasingly heavy taxes, complemented by offers from the Ghetto itself, which, through the mouths of its leaders, constantly had to acknowledge the force of an incontrovertible "political reason". This tug of war was settled in 1537 by agreement on a sum of 13.000 ducats, part imposition and part gift from the Jews, but it broke out again several times over the ensuing centuries, always with similar outcomes. One effect of this, however, was that the newly installed community acquired a greater guarantee of stability and internal security. From that time until 1571, the residence rights of the German "nation" were never seriously debated, nor was the precise social function it was destined to fulfill.

In the first half of the 16th century, most of the Jews in the Ghetto were Ashkenazim (from the Hebrew 'ashkenazi — German) who had been living for some time in Veneto territory, following the stream of migrants from central and eastern Europe caused mainly by savage anti-Semitic persecutions which had destroyed hundreds of communities large and small and provoked dramatic slaughter and havoc. In fact, the living conditions of the German Jews in the late Middle Ages had been very hard. Surrounded by widespread anti-Semitism, often dependent on the whim of individual local rulers or imperial authorities, barred from any commercial or industrial association, often constrained to change abode because of violent eruptions of hatred, they had been obliged by circumstance to devote themselves exclusively to retailing or moneylending. Their situation had worsened since 1298, when a nobleman from Röttingen in Franconia had begun spreading damaging accusations about their profaning the Host, which set off vast persecutions that soon reached Bavaria and Austria and led to the destruction of hundreds of entire communities. But their lives had been turned into complete tragedy during the terrible plagues of 1348-50, when people accused the Jews of actually contaminating wells and deliberately spreading the cruel contagion out of revenge. Interventions by both the Emperor and the Church were powerless to avert the mad wave of anti-Semitic fanaticism which broke out in murders and massacres in many communities, obliging all those not disposed to compulsory conversion to flee and seek refuge in more hospitable, or at least not overtly hostile lands. Thus, between the 13th and 14th centuries, many German moneylenders or traders had flooded into northern Italy, scattered from Trieste to Lombardy, but mainly occupying inland towns in the Veneto region, such as Bassano, Treviso and Ceneda, across to the lagoon district, Mestre in particular, whence they fled to seek refuge in Venice.

Although the German "nation" was the only group to deal directly with the State, at least the only one cited in official documents — while Venetians and rich Levantine merchants undoubtedly had dwellings in their *campo* during their stays (Ravid) —, it must be remembered that there were other groups of Jews living inside, the so-called "Italian" immigrants from central and southern Italy. From their main concentration in the Rome area, which had for centuries been the oldest Jewish community in Italy, but coming also from the south, particularly after the anti-Semitic campaign of the late 13th century, they began to push north during the 13th and 14th centuries, not in great migratory waves, but rather in

small family groups, usually motivated by economic reasons to practise moneylending in cities and small towns. Little by little the *condotta* was drawn up for the various bankers, which guaranteed them a secure existence. From Tuscany to Umbria, from the Marches to Emilia and Veneto, they formed what history refers to officially as the "ascending current" of Roman money-lenders, which in Veneto mingled with the tide of Germans, while still remaining in the minority, to form the ethnic basis of the new Venetian community. Differing from the Germans in their rituals, the Italian Jews in Venice never constituted an independent "nation" and were always lumped together with the Ashkenazim, sharing their conditions and situations, occupations and professions, but always remaining inferior in number and wealth, though not in cultural quality or religious devotion.

22

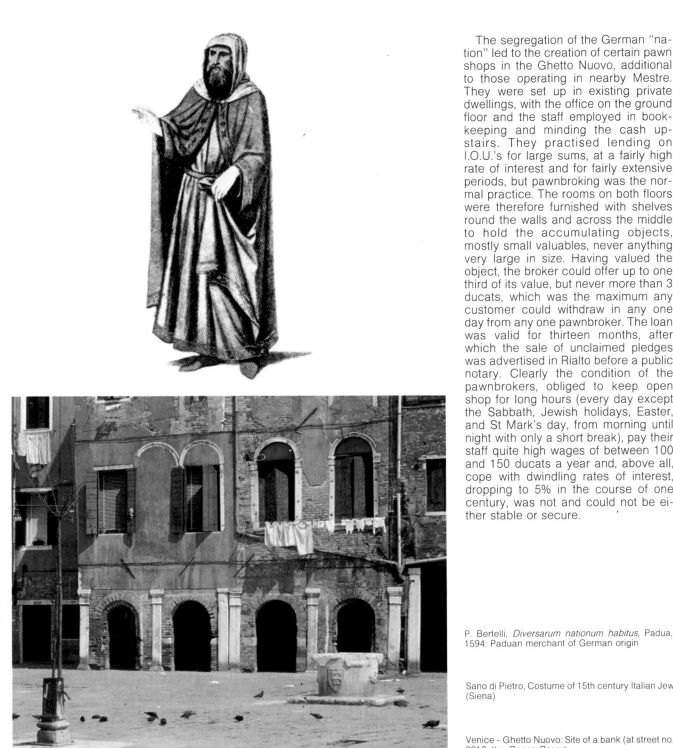

The segregation of the German "nation" led to the creation of certain pawn shops in the Ghetto Nuovo, additional to those operating in nearby Mestre. They were set up in existing private dwellings, with the office on the ground floor and the staff employed in bookkeeping and minding the cash upstairs. They practised lending on I.O.U.'s for large sums, at a fairly high rate of interest and for fairly extensive periods, but pawnbroking was the normal practice. The rooms on both floors were therefore furnished with shelves round the walls and across the middle to hold the accumulating objects, mostly small valuables, never anything very large in size. Having valued the object, the broker could offer up to one third of its value, but never more than 3 ducats, which was the maximum any customer could withdraw in any one day from any one pawnbroker. The loan was valid for thirteen months, after which the sale of unclaimed pledges was advertised in Rialto before a public notary. Clearly the condition of the pawnbrokers, obliged to keep open shop for long hours (every day except the Sabbath, Jewish holidays, Easter, and St Mark's day, from morning until night with only a short break), pay their staff quite high wages of between 100 and 150 ducats a year and, above all, cope with dwindling rates of interest, dropping to 5% in the course of one century, was not and could not be either stable or secure.

23

P. Bertelli, *Diversarum nationum habitus*, Padua, 1594: Paduan merchant of German origin

Sano di Pietro, Costume of 15th century Italian Jew (Siena)

Venice - Ghetto Nuovo: Site of a bank (at street no. 2912: the *Banco Rosso*)

The choice between Monti di Pietà and Jewish lending was argued with mounting fervour during the 1520's. Meanwhile, the Venetian Jews played a leading part in two episodes with international implications, revealing the importance they had already assumed even beyond Italy. In 1524, while going through a troubled period, shaken by religious fervour and hopes of redemption, the Venetian community itself was the cradle for the "false Messiah" Dawidh Reubeni, one of the many who appeared in Europe during the history of the Diaspora. About the same time, Venetian rabbis were among the first to hold discussions with Henry VIII on the tricky question of his second marriage, which was to result in the Church of England's breakaway from Rome.

24 The mysterious figure of Dawidh Reubeni first landed in Venice in 1524, after a long series of journeys in the Middle East. He was a strange but fascinating person of Ethiopian origin, probably a Falashan (U. Cassuto), inclined towards asceticism, but with a tendency to recount fantastic tales. Introduced by the famous painter Mosheh da Castellazzo, he was favourably received by the Ghetto leaders, and told them how he was descended from the ancient tribe of Re'ubhen, was a brother of King Joseph, then ruling in Palestine, and had been sent to gather forces and weapons, both Jewish and Christian, for a decisive battle against the Turks. Inspired by his revelations, the yearning for redemption and the possibility of returning to their homeland quickly spread in minds particularly disposed towards messianic overtures in the newly created *campo*, and funds were readily collected to send the Ethiopian on a journey to Rome, where Pope Clement VII evidently made him very welcome in the Vatican, and another to the King of Portugal — where the enthusiasm he aroused among the converts from Judaism persuaded a young officer to reconvert and, under the name of Solomon Molcho, become an actively enthusiastic redemptionist —, and finally to bring him back to Venice in 1530. The chronicler Marin Sanuto recounts that Reubeni was then lodged

in the house of Count Guido Rangon at San Patrinian "in chà Contarini" — probably the famous Contarini del Bovolo Palace with its celebrated spiral staircase built by Candi in the late 15th century (Di Segni) — where, on instructions from the Senate, the famous voyager was questioned by G.B. Ramusio, who immediately confirmed the suspicions that had begun to seep around Europe about such fantastic promises. Dawidh seemed to him an eccentric person, his plans and propaganda "fixations of the brain"; in short, there were grave doubts about the new prophet's sanity. He was defended by the well known doctor Elia Halfon, and the doubts were openly contradicted by the still better known Jacob Mantino, but the discrediting of the false redeemer's activity began to spread round the Ghetto, his career declined towards ul-

timate disaster, and the hopes and enthusiasm of an entire community slowly dissolved, as would those aroused by the Shabbetai Tzebhi Movement and various resurrectionist proposals a century and a half later.

In those same years (1527-33), against the general disappointment that permeated the Ashkenazic core, the learned rabbis of the Ghetto won the proud satisfaction of finding themselves at the centre of one of the most important events of contemporary history, destined, as a primary consequence, to force the schism between Rome and the Anglican Church, but also to bring cultural prestige to the Jewish community, which was to stand on the Lagoon for centuries. Henry VIII of England had for some time been on the road to a break from Rome, and to effect his policy he used the pretext that his mar-

riage to his brother Arthur's widow, Catherine of Aragon (and aunt to Emperor Charles V), was invalid according to the Bible (*Leviticus* XX, 21) and the Canons of the Church, proved by the fact that he had no male heir. He therefore asked Pope Clement VII for permission to marry Anne Boleyn. But according to the rite of *yibbum* and the Bible, principally *Deuteronomy* XXV, a man is actually obliged to marry his brother's widow if he has died without heirs able to carry on the family name, and this created a difficult obstacle to surmount if a peaceable solution were to be reached. To settle this delicate controversy King Henry not only appealed to the bishops and the Pope, but sent his representative Richard Croke to consult the rabbis and Jewish scholars of Venice, some of whom, excluding Jacob Mantino, again through the mouth

of Elia Halfon, actually decided in support of the English thesis. It was naturally of little importance that these few were contradicted by the majority of Italian rabbis and flouted at the time by a marriage in Bologna between a man and his brother's widow, in keeping with Hebrew custom. What was important here, as in the other episode, was the credit directly reflected on Jewish culture in Venice. Many, in fact, have seen this as the start of the repropagation of rabbinical literature in Europe, others of the reflourishing of Talmudic and Biblical studies, but in the event it should rather be seen against the background of the climate of redemption then being experienced in the Venetian Ghetto, above all, a will to survive within their tradition, all the more admirable when placed against the painful state of recently imposed segregation.

Venice - Ghetto Nuovo: Campo di Ghetto Nuovo (detail)

◀Venice - Contarini Palace: The Spiral Staircase (the *Bovolo*) attributed to G. Candi (1499)

The first and most conspicuous sign that the German Jews' situation was settling down was the building of two Ashkenazic synagogues, the *Scola Grande Tedesca* in 1528-29 and the *Scola Canton* in 1531-32. They were to become the nerve centres of the entire community life.

Since the destruction of the Temple, the synagogue had assumed a progressively vast range of functions, making it quite different from the Christian church. It was not only the *Beyth Keneseth* — "meeting house" — for gathering and the saying of public prayers, but also the *Beyth midhrash* — "study house" — for daily reading and study of the *Torah*, and the place of assembly and coordination of the whole administrative apparatus of every single Jewish group. So the synagogue building, which the Jews themselves called *scola,* "school" (Greek *scholé*), in the sense of "brotherhood, congregation" had been constructed as a complex of spacious and flexible rooms around the central prayer hall, individually adapted to the various daily functions of the *qahal qadhosh* — "holy community" — in a way unlike any other religious edifice. In common with every other aspect of Jewish art, however, the architectural style and the interior decoration, though distinctive in their way, did not show a recognizably independent conception of space and never revealed features of true originality. They were often, in fact, the result of a slow assimilation of the dominant characteristics of the artistic cultures of the various countries of the Diaspora and their adaptation to the demands of Jewish religious tradition, always respecting the customs of orientation and the standards imposed by the *halakhah* — the section of Talmudic writings dealing with law and ritual. In many cases the results were highly accomplished.

Being isolated behind closed walls, each ethnic group gradually formed a *qehillah* — "community" — developing a spirit determined to maintain distinct customs and traditions supported of course by an appropriate administrative organization, which could only take shape within the synagogue. This tended to be reinforced with buildings consistently designed to preserve patterns already consolidated. And since "the style of worship is very different between . . . nations, in fact there is no way in which they distinguish themselves one from another more than this" to the extent that "each . . . wants one (synagogue) in its own style" (Leon Modena), it was a logical consequence that the Ashkenazi group should have immediately erected their culturally distinct buildings to guarantee and preserve their own cultural and religious heritage. Thus, barely fifteen years after the Ghetto was closed in, rose two of the finest synagogues in Venice.

Maḥazor of the German ritual (Venice - 1568), book of prayers for feastdays

26

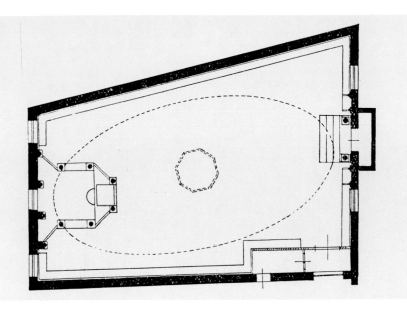

Interior of an ancient synagogue (14th C.)

The·*Scola Grande Tedesca* is the most striking product of the integration between the community's historical memory of their central European building traditions and architectural design ideas from Italian synagogues in Venice. It was originally structured according to the criteria of simplicity and functionality typical of Ashkenazi work, inserted, necessarily, in already existent buildings in order to remain hidden from strangers' eyes, positioned above other rooms according to the Halakhic exhortation to place the synagogues in the highest part of cities, and distinguished on the outside only by the "signal" of the five windows. In time the Germans' prayer hall underwent some transformation, the interior becoming ever more richly decorated, and the architectural dimensions being modified, in a gradual adaptation to western examples present in the Ghetto.

It was built in 5289 (1529) — according to the plaque set over the five windows on the façade — on the upper floor of a two-storey building, in a limited space that strictly determined the internal planning and the structural harmony. In its original design it showed typically Ashkenazi characteristics. The *bimah* (dais) was in the middle of the hall, not to one side, as in the bifocal plan recurrent in the Italian area, the marble wall-cladding showed an obvious central European derivation, the benches for worshippers were probably set parallel to the short sides, and the women's gallery was probably on the small rostrum before the entrance door. A feature quite unique in Veneto was the continuous frieze all round the inside, bearing the Ten Commandments in gold letters on a red ground, not only having a decorative function but being an integrating part of the architectural ensemble. Entrance, according to Cassuto's theory, was by way of a long, steep staircase leading up directly from the ground floor to the prayer hall.

This arrangement, however, was modified in various ways at different times until it reached the form in which it survives today. First, it was panelled with wood, with benches along the walls, according to the custom even in Venetian meeting and study halls, and the triple structure of the '*aron* (Ark of the Covenant) was inserted in the mid 17th century, bringing concrete changes. But without doubt the most radical modification occurred in the early 18th century, altering the building's appearance in the course of adaptation to ideas from other synagogues in Venice. The complete inscription on the plaque above the windows says that "*when the building was founded it was 5289 (1529) and at its construction for the second time the date was 5493 (1733)*" (Cassuto). In fact those were the years when there were restorations in all the Ghetto's "scole" and this date can certainly be attributed to the horizontal division of the entire construction into four floors, readapting the stairs and permitting the later insertion of the oval women's gallery inside the prayer hall, demanding an entire spatial reorganization. Finally, the 19th century removal of the *bimah* onto the short side opposite the '*aron*, necessitating the closure of two of the five windows and giving the hall a bifocal arrangement, eliminated the last Ashkenazic accent to persist since its origin. Through successive restorations in 1848 (according to the plaque on the first landing of the staircase), 1860 (Ottolenghi), 1910 (Morpurgo), and most recently 1975-79, the Ghetto's oldest and arguably finest synagogue has managed to maintain its former integrity and preserve the solemn atmosphere of contemplation that has always distinguished it.

As always, the synagogue building is not very conspicuous from outside. It is distinguished from its neighbours only by the motif of five white-arched windows, two now bricked up, and the modest portal recently inserted into a structure reminiscent of the nearby Scola Italiana. Its white stone arch bears the inscription: "*Grand temple according to the Ashkenazi rite*" echoed in another inscription under the cornice of the adjacent, higher section of the building: "*Grand scola (temple) of the sacred community of Germans by the protection of God. Amen*". One plaque above the five windows records, as we have seen, the essential dates in the building's history, while the second, in accordance with the custom for all public buildings, commemorates the destruction of the Temple of Jerusalem.

The present stairs, which replaced the previous single steep flight (Cassuto), were restored in 5608 (1848), according to the inscription in the centre of the first landing, and lead to what used to be the old synagogue's service or meeting rooms, but now house the modern Museum of Hebrew Art.

Along the walls are many commemorative or celebratory inscriptions from various periods. One tablet in 19th century Italian verse, similar to one now beside the upper entrance to the nearby Scola Canton, addresses those going to pray in the prayer hall, exhorting them to purity: "*Shed, mortal Man, all wicked, black intent / When towards Temple worship thy feet move; / Think whom thou prayest, and with faithful love / Let all thy mind be on the Divine Subject bent*".

The plan of the actual prayer hall is a highly asymmetrical transverse trapezium; the original builder and subsequent renovators have had to resort to various expedients and novel strategies to achieve an intimate and unified interior. The entrance door is in a corner, a most unusual position compared with traditional synagogue layouts, and succeeds in averting any sense of disharmony in first impressions of the interior. But it is principally the interior colour scheme and traditional decorative motifs, added to over the years, that firmly ensure the impression of a unified whole. The wooden panelling and balco-

Venice - Ghetto Nuovo: Scola Grande Tedesca, Façade on the "campo"

28

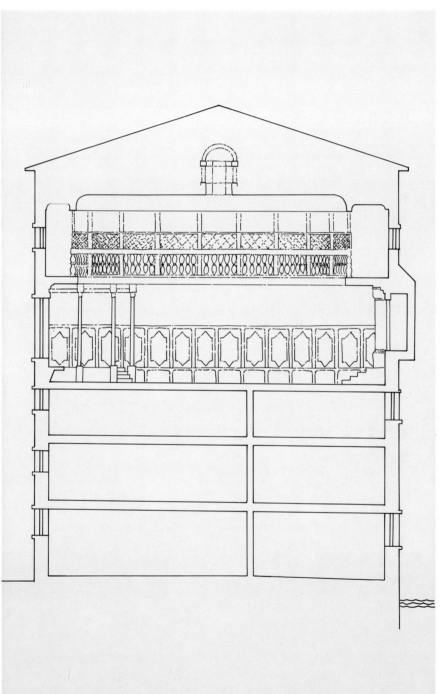

nies, decorated with pilasters and projecting polygonal bosses, the upper walls clad with variegated marble, and the red frieze bearing the Ten Commandments from *Exodus* (Yithro) XX, 2-17, going right round and linking the perimeter walls, combine to create a sense of varied homogeneity.

Similarly, the short sides are linked by the arrangement of the prayer benches — probably 16th century and without doubt the oldest features of all the furnishings —, which accentuates the room's twin focus created when the *bimah* was resited. The elliptical women's gallery, adorned with a balustrade with stylized late baroque columns, hardly fits into the space left by the early one, which was perhaps originally fixed to the long entrance wall, but successfully confers an illusion of dignified symmetry on the room. The underlying decorative idea of this structure was perhaps suggested by a similar one in the Scola Spagnola, and may have something to do with the oval boxes in Venetian theatres (Cassuto). The constant use of circular and rectangular motifs in its oval crown, repeating those present both in the *bimah* and in the ornamental frieze on the ceiling (renovated in 1860), suggests a close web of internal echoes, establishing a deeper connection between the parts. Finally, the gilding, applied to single items of the whole ensemble, fixtures or furniture, combines excellently with the scarlet of the curtains and draperies; both recall the divine choice imposed on the ancient *Mishkan*, the desert Tabernacle (*Exodus* XXVI-XXVII). Their effective contribution fulfils the aim that the architectural structure alone would not have been able to achieve.

29

Venice - Ghetto Nuovo: Scola Grande Tedesca, Prayer hall (section)

There seems to have been a similar, if not completely successful, intention behind the decorative outlines of the two focal points in the hall, apart from the colour schemes, which are suitably balanced. The clearest example is the stylistic similarity between the entrance door and the articulated parts of the *'aron*. The Ark of the Covenant is situated towards Jerusalem and stands before a niche on the short side of the hall which, under the evident influence of the Venetian *liagò* (sun balcony) projects over the Rio di Ghetto Nuovo. Flanked by two large windows, it takes the form of a triple structure, perhaps reminiscent of altars in Venetian churches; it was installed in a later period than the marble wall cladding and the ornamental red frieze which it partially obscures. The central section rests on a high, decorated plinth, framed by fluted Corinthian columns that support a baroque architrave adorned with vases and cornucopias. The doors of the cupboard that houses the *Sepharim* (scrolls of the Law) are decorated on the inside with the Ten Commandments inlaid in mother-of-pearl and, on the outside, with a beautifully stylized Tree of Life. To raise it above the general level of the hall, it is preceded by four steps, the top one bearing a Hebrew inscription that says: "*(Gift) from the eldest of the Zemel brothers, the Rabbi Menaḥem Cividale, son of the Rabbi Joseph Zemel, in the year 5432 (Tzaddiq wenosha'hu'* — May the just be saved)". The date corresponds to 1672 and may refer to the time either of construction or of interior restoration. The two stalls on either side match the central structure in both style and exquisite workmanship, so it is highly probable that they date from the same year. Any worshipper could buy his own seat in the hall and pass it on to his heirs. These two probably belonged to the two *parnasim*, the wardens and general administrators of the synagogue, who were elected annually by the General Assembly, according to two ancient manuscripts of 1611 and 1649 about rules and inventories, now lost (Ottolenghi). Under their direction, in strict hierarchy, operated the other elected officials, the secretaries (*gabba'im*), the men responsible for lamp lighting (*parnas 'al shemen lama-'or*) and for collecting the offerings for the Holy Land (*gabbay*), the treasurer (*gizbar*), the officiant, cantor and musical director (*ḥazzan*) and the sexton (*shammash*).

In the decoration on the high backs of the stalls, two verses from the Bible stress the wisdom and maturity of judgement that should guide those with a leading responsibility for the religious house: (right) "*Ubhmoshabh zeqenim yehaleluhu — And praise Him in the seat of the elders*" (*Psalm* CVII, 32) and (left) "*Yoshebh bashshebheth taḥke-mon(i) — He who sits in the assembly shall become wise*" recalling *Samuel II*, XXIII, 8-9, which cites the first of the *gibborim*, "the mighty men whom David had".

Venice - Ghetto Nuovo: Scola Grande Tedesca, the 'aron

Venice - Ghetto Nuovo: Scola Grande Tedesca, the bimah

The *bimah* is less successfully integrated with the architectural ensemble. It is certain that, originally, the officiant's dais was situated according to Ashkenazic custom in the centre of the hall, in the daylight from the octagonal lantern opened in the ceiling directly above. This is confirmed by analysing the floor decoration, which is in the form of large rosettes, but with a blank space in the middle that can only be plausibly explained by assuming that it was formerly covered by one of the hall's two focal points. In the process of gradual adaptation to local custom, the *bimah* was moved against the short wall opposite the 'aron, which meant bricking up two windows, interrupting the decorative wall cladding and the inscription above, and adapting awkwardly to the elliptical women's gallery. Exactly when this was done is hard to say. It is certain only that it happened after the gates of the Ghetto were pulled down in the 19th century, not during the great 18th century restoration. In 1796, in fact, two of the Scola's congregation complained before the Officials of the *Cattaver* about the discomfort of those who had their places on the benches under the five windows giving onto the Campo del Ghetto Nuovo; according to their testimony the light and the rain seeping in were a nuisance to the faithful during prayers (Carletto). Beyond that it is impossible to say whether the present arrangement dates back to the early 19th century or the 1860 restoration (Ottolenghi), when the *bimah* itself was adapted to the wall by being modified from octagonal to trapezoidal, losing some of its original grace in the process. Today it projects boldly from the back wall, standing on a plinth decorated with the same geometric motif as the ceiling, with a balustrade of very effective gilded banisters, on which stand eight slender stylized Corinthian columns supporting a light entablature embellished with vases like those on the 'aron. The ornamental elements admittedly succeed in linking the overall decorative scheme, while the structural solutions suggest a sense of airy composure, but it is undeniable that the hall's original proportions, already precarious in themselves, have not been in any way improved by these modifications, however adroit.

Not far from the Scola Grande Tedesca stands the *Scola Canton*, built only three years later. It too is cleverly inser-

31

ted into the top storey of an existing building where it is almost invisible from outside, and is certainly the most perfect of all Venetian synagogues in the harmonious symmetry of its lines and the calculated refinement of its decoration. It is not easy to find documentary evidence, but the new synagogue was very likely needed because the Scola Grande was not big enough for the great number of Jews enclosed in the Ghetto, or it may have been that a small group of Ashkenazim coming from a different area from the majority, although belonging to the German *minhagh* (ritual), wished to preserve a distinct ritual. The name *Santa Comunità Canton*, which appears on the outer portal together with the date the synagogue was built, seems to be not a simple topographical allusion to the siting of the building in a *corner* of the Campo di Ghetto Nuovo (in Venetian *cantón* means *corner*), but a reference to the surname, Cantoni, of a family, or rather an interrelated group of families, who built their own private *scola* in order to follow a separate ritual. This theory would seem to be confirmed by certain liturgical differences between the rituals followed in the two synagogues (for example, the 16th century Cabalistic, acrostic hymn of S. Alqabez Halewi, "*Lekhah dhodhi — Come, my delight*" sung at the Friday evening service, is not included in the prayers of the Scola Grande Tedesca), while the very eccentricity of choosing a bifocal plan, which is against established central European tradition, would seem to credit it with no less well founded motivation. It could in fact indicate a derivation not so much from earlier Italian models as from building conventions widespread in southern France, and so suggest the unconfirmed but not wholly strange assumption of a group of Ashkenazim of French origin (Cassuto) who wanted, in this way, to assert and maintain their own spiritual identity and religious customs.

32

The hymn *Lekhah dhodhi* (from the *Sepher ha-maphṭir* of Urbino, 1704)

From the beginning, in fact, this synagogue was planned with two focal points, similar to the nearby Scola Grande in the location and general arrangement of its various functional and decorative features, but solving all its space problems with such technical brilliance as to far outshine its nobler companion in harmony of composition and inner composure. As the building stands today, its late baroque style with touches of early rococo — net result of various renovations over the years — in no way detracts from the exquisite lines of the prayer hall. A small inscription, low down to the left of the *bimah*, marking an offering by one Shlomoh of 180 ducats for his own house of worship, records that it was built in 5292 (1531-32). The hall of the synagogue is an almost regular oblong with the *'aron* and the *bimah* at either end and the pews for the worshippers straight down the long sides, linking the two focal points and leaving a wide space in between. The characteristic five windows are placed in the long wall opposite the entrance, and in the door wall itself there are corresponding, symmetrical openings through to the small vestibule, perhaps designed as a rudimentary women's gallery (Cassuto). Over the centuries it has undergone many adaptations, but nothing has changed its original character.

According to Leon Modena, the side rooms were first extended in 1639 at the request of the *parnasim* (wardens) of the time, Baldoza, Cervi, Kohen and Kohen Porto, but the main hall escaped attention. A major alteration was carried out only about thirty years later, when the entire set of the *'aron* and the two stalls for dignitaries was installed in front of the existing walls, probably occasioning fresh decoration. The complete decorative scheme of the interior grew to its finished state throughout the 18th century, its phases marked by various inscriptions. Early in the century, the walls of the apsidiole behind the *bimah* were lined with wood panelling, while in about 1730, when extensive restorations were going on in all the Ghetto synagogues, the foundation probably underwent its most radical facelift. There is an inscription on the cornice of the entrance door, in the small frieze above the ornamental shell and below it, which says that about 5496 (1736), on the wishes of the *parnasim* De Cervi, Capon, Clerle, Parenzo and Baldoza, the walls were repanelled, the floor and ceiling designs were completed, and two basic features of the entire complex were probably installed, the *bimah*, or at least its supporting structures, and the women's gallery, from this time on located on a higher level and perfectly camouflaged by the geometric shapes of the partition wall, with the consequent transformation of the little vestibule opening on the hall into a room for the poor or a simple waiting room (Cassuto). The interior was then gilded, spreading a uniform patina over the already compact structural harmony; according to the inscription above the entrance portal, between the central inlaid panel and a small fluted wooden frieze, it was completed by the "Santa Comunità Canton" in 5540 (1780) at the end of *'Elul* (September-October) by way of ornament "to honour the House of the Lord". In 5607 (1847), according to the inscription on the panel above the wide arch of the *bimah*, there followed the last modifications, including the closure of the aperture remaining between the main hall and the vestibule and the consequent extension of the decorative scheme over the south wall, resulting in the definitive uniformity that still distinguishes the exquisite little Ashkenazi school. Postwar restorations, continued in 1983, have given absolute priority to preserving this unity.

33

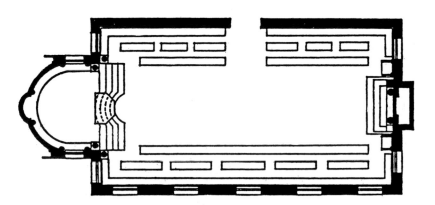

Venice - Ghetto Nuovo: Scola Canton, Floorplan
(12.90m x 7.10m x 12.75m x 6.50m)

From outside, the synagogue is quite inconspicuous, easily confused with the surrounding houses. The rules of layout and direction have in fact meant that the five-window motif is on the wall overlooking the canal instead of facing onto the Campo di Ghetto Nuovo. All the same, it is distinguishable by the small entrance portal in the corner of the square — the arch bearing the dates when it was founded and when the stairs were completely rebuilt (5619-1859) — and above all by the eccentric little umbrella-shaped cupola resting on an octagonal lantern which, as in the nearby Scola Italiana, lets light down onto the apsidiole of the *bimah*, clad on the outside with wooden boarding. When the present staircase replaced the old steeper one in the 19th century it caused radical changes in the interior layout of the rooms (Cassuto). In height, the two floors flanking the prayer hall have each been divided into four, which has made space for offices, entrance hall, a room for the poor and, level with the women's gallery, a *sukkah* (the "tabernacle" in which it is obligatory to reside during the autumn feast of *Sukkoth*, in memory of the tabernacles the Jews built in the desert after the exodus from Egypt — *Leviticus* XXIII, 33-43), obviously without a roof, but covered with a wooden screen, movable so that it can be left open to the sky as the rule dictates. On the top landing there is a modest doorway above which, in 5602 (1842), J. Fano had placed an inscription similar to that in the Scola Grande Tedesca (*Sgombra, o mortal . . — Shed, mortal man...*); it leads into a small oblong vestibule with benches round the walls, which in the original design probably acted as the women's gallery, in contact with the prayer hall through four wide openings, then during the 18th century restoration was transformed into a lecture room for worshippers, and finally, with the late 19th century alterations, became a simple waiting room and meeting place with no specific function. Above the entrance into the main prayer hall a small tablet bearing a verse from *Proverbs* VIII, 34 reminds those who enter of the value of faith and daily prayer: " *'ashrey 'adham shomea' li lishqodh 'al-dalthothay yom yom — Blessed is the man that heareth me, watching daily at my gates*". Above the door on the opposite side is a message to those leaving: "*We 'atah shubh we-lekh leshalom welo' ta'aśeh ra' — Arise now, go in peace and do no evil*".

34

Venice - Ghetto Nuovo: Scola Canton, exterior on the campo

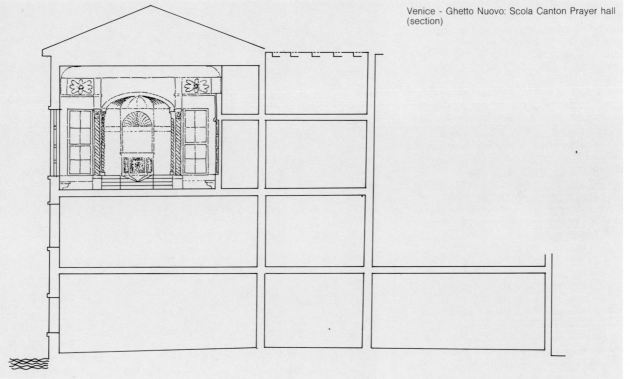

The prayer hall is an almost square rectangle, owing its interior unity and composure to the detailed integration between wall structure and decorative features. The row of five windows looking onto the Rio di Ghetto Nuovo to some extent supplies the unifying motif of the entire complex, steering the ornamental scheme on a constant line of internal echoes. According to the characteristic bifocal plan, the hall's two focal points are linked not only by the benches running along the side walls, which are wood-panelled two thirds of the way up, and by parallel rows of pews for worshippers — leaving a wide space in the middle paved with "Venetian terrazzo" dominated by a circular ornament with geometrical insertions — but also, and most effectively, by two decorative friezes, a series of similar panels which create a mood of compact uniformity, and succeed in establishing an unusually beautiful five-section rhythm over the entire wall area.

The two longer walls are horizontally divided into five unequal parts by carefully positioned and completely functional sliding windows in place of the original openings of the women's gallery, surmounted by two series of panels with cut-out oval geometric patterns and inlaid decorative motifs, leaving space on the south wall for Biblical scenes showing Moses striking water from the rock, the crossing of the Red Sea, and the sacrificial altar at Jerusalem.

Vertically, the two sides are divided into sections, windows alternating with wooden panels carved into relief motifs in late baroque-rococo style, adorned with three-branched candelabra of more modern period, which lead the eye up to the ceiling, linked in turn to the decorations below by a simple cornice of marble festoons, restored in the early 18th century. The ornamental rhythm is interrupted only by the scallop-shell coping over the main door, its top frame

bearing the date 1736 and the names of the wardens who restored the hall, and by the slab above it bearing a text from *Deuteronomy* X, 12: "*We'atah yiśra'el mah'A. 'eloheykha sho'el me'immakh... — And now, Israel, what doth the Lord thy God require of thee, but to fear the Lord thy God, to walk in all His ways, and to love Him, and to serve the Lord thy God with all thy heart and with all thy soul?*". Three final letters are missing, however, from three words on the last two lines. Until the latest restoration, this original inscription was covered by a verse from *Kings I*, VIII, 30, which has now been removed.

Once again, however, it is the hall's two focal points, with their perfectly balanced proportions, that complete the refined composure of the total ensemble. Each fits into a perfect semicircle whose diameter corresponds to the entire width of the hall (Cassuto) and, although belonging to different periods, they impart a sense of lightness and elegance that blends closely with the synagogue's serene atmosphere. The *'aron*, much like the one in the Scola Grande Tedesca, is in three parts, fitting neatly into pre-existing wall structures and uniting with the ornamental decorations to achieve a rhythm over the whole wall of five unequal sections, which immediately harmonizes with the unifying motif of the overall scheme. It has magnificent doors inlaid and gilded on the outside (after *Exodus XXXVII, 2*) and engraved with the *Kether Torah* (Crown of the Torah) above the Ten Commandments on the inside, and is flanked by two Corinthian columns on bases and two pilasters supporting a heavily ornamented pediment pierced in the centre by a bright stained glass window of fan-shaped design, striking a most effective note of colour. Its 17th century style design is repeated in the two wardens' stalls, flanked by half-columns, their lower part spiralled and the upper fluted, on either side of the central section and surmounted by similar, smaller pediments, which are effectively complementary. The two side tablets bear two prayers for (left) the ending of the Sabbath: *I' 'atah ḥonantanu - Thou hast granted us* and (right) the Sabbath of solemn feast: *Watodhi-'enu - And thou hast given us to know* while the central two, now lost, used to represent the Tablets of the Law. Their luminary effect, piercing the mystic twilight that bathes the Ark of the Covenant in contrast to the surrounding halo of light from the two windows, satisfies a typically baroque taste for chiaroscuro. The structure is approached by four steps on which is written a dedication in skilful colour contrast with the surrounding gilding: *"Gift of Yehushua' Mosheh for the rest of his brother decapitated like an animal / The day of his birth was a sorry day for him. In his 44th year may*

his blood be before God a sacrificial offering: Mordekhay b. Menaḥem Baldoza, the fourth day (Wednesday) 9 Nisan; and he was buried the second day (Monday) 26 'iyyar in the year 5432 (1672). (qibbel berahami(m) 'A. — thou receivest with mercy O Lord)". The inscription is complex in detail and somewhat difficult to interpret, but it may point to a probable dating.

Venice - Ghetto Nuovo: Scola Canton, the *'aron*

Venice - Ghetto Nuovo: Scola Canton, the *bimah* ▶

The *bimah*, of a remarkable and highly effective design that is repeated in various ways in other Venetian synagogues, stands against the opposite wall in a raised position, rhythmically dividing the entire wall, once again, into five clear sections. Its original beauty and refined scheme of decoration suggest an approximately late 18th century dating. A small polygonal pulpit, finely decorated with geometric reliefs, is poised in a concave space bounded by five wooden steps, which raise it above the level of the hall. It is framed by a very fine semi-elliptical arch (inscribed with the restoration date of 1846-47) supported by two pairs of original pierced columns with stems of intertwined branches, which circumscribes a wide polygonal apsidiole. This is an eccentric structure with two side windows

and, round the walls, wood panelling with benches interrupted in the middle by a seat in a niche under a scallop-shell hood, the gift, so the inscription tells us, "*of Beniamino Marina di Conselve: may His Rock defend him and keep him alive*".

The cupola opening in the ceiling, surrounded by areas of background colour, enhances the whole spatial concept. As mentioned, a small stone low down on the left, recording the offering of one Shlomoh for the building of the synagogue, carries the date of its founding, the same as is indicated on the entrance portal in the Campo di Ghetto Nuovo.

The building of the two Ashkenazi synagogues around which the life of the Ghetto revolved enabled the Jews to recite their three daily prayers in public, take part in the traditional morning lesson and sermon and, most importantly, attend the reading of the Torah, thus leading to a revival of their cult. But this was not all. It also provided a fresh incentive to cultural and scientific development along traditional lines, and it is surely here that we can recognize the most intelligent and constructive response on the part of the Jewish community to the discrimination they suffered from outside. Around the Scola Grande Tedesca, in almost idealistic furtherance of the late 15th century activity of the famous Yehudhah Mintz's celebrated *yeshibhah* (Talmudic academy) in Padua, a group of rabbis with a deep commitment to doctrine set to work to study the Law and its interpretation, and gave it a moderate conservationist reading so precise that it remained for a long time the guiding tract for all the Ashkenazi intelligentsia. In principle, they anchored themselves firmly to traditional Talmudism and aimed at keeping intact the German *minhagh* (ritual), at the same time preserving Yiddish, the German-Hebrew dialect, which was becoming adulterated by contact with the local dialect; but they were careful never in any way to discourage inquiring interest expressed towards Judaism by non-Jewish scholars and worshippers, nor reject cautious and measured open-mindedness towards the mystic currents within their own Jewish culture. The presence of a man like 'Abhraham de Balmes, an illustrious doctor and astrologer, author of a grammar constructed on the application of Cabalistic methodology (Bomberg, Venice 1523), and the publication, also in 1523 by the same Bomberg, of the Cabalistic commentary to the first five books of the Old Testament by Menahem da Recanati and S. Saba, show the existence of a curiosity, albeit intellectual and elitist, about mystic and esoteric tendencies present in Judaism (Bonfil). Moreover, the expert translation of philosophical and scientific works carried out by illustrious doctors

37

like Calonimos and Mantino, who had always enjoyed privileged treatment from *La Serenissima*, in spite of their segregation in the Ghetto, demonstrates their inclination towards a fruitful collaboration with the more advanced section of Venetian culture.

In such a climate, when great minds within the Ghetto such as Elia Levita, Ya'aqobh ben Ḥayyim and Me'ir Parenzo, themselves attracted by the prestige of the Venetian milieu, were allied with the strong and typically humanistic interest in Judaism evinced by Christian intellectuals and culturalists, certainly the most conspicuous fruit of these particularly favourable circumstances was the flourishing and dissemination of printed Hebrew literature, which, availing itself of most worthy Ashkenazi experts and collections of important manuscripts such as that of Cardinal Grimani, placed Venice, for a short time, at the peak of European publishing.

The early 16th century was marked not only by the publication of works responding specifically to the conservationist demands of the "German nation" from the *maḥazor* (forms of prayer for festivities) to the *Ma'asim* (tales of Yiddish tradition), but also by the publishing of Judaism's basic texts, which were philologically quite thorough and, in some cases, definitive, from the Bible, the *Mishnah* and the *Talmudh* to the morality tales of the various *midhrashim*. These were aimed not only at Jews wishing to perpetuate their ethical and religious heritage, but also at a non-Jewish public wishing to consult the authentic originals of works so important to the history of Western culture. According to explicit declarations in the dedications or colophons of many volumes, the devotion of the scholars at the Scola Grande Tedesca to what came to be known as their *mele'kheth qodhesh* (sacred work), their philological care and sometimes their definition of texts in the more reliable manuscripts, was then of major importance. Restrictions imposed by the authorities prevented Jews from printing in their own names, and the entire process, at least in the early decades of the century, depended primarily on a sincere

literary interest on the part of non-Jewish personalities, over and above possible commercial profits, but the contribution of Jewish doctrine in all the preparatory phases up to proof correction was such that these 16th century editions, although benefitting from unsurpassed typographical characters, would never have achieved the model quality that distinguishes them had they been brought out independently of the cultural atmosphere generated in the Venetian Ghetto in its early years.

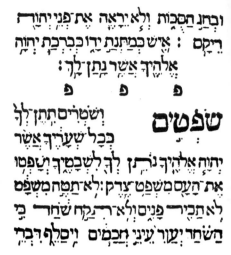

Characters used by Soncino (1492), the greatest Hebrew printer in Italy before Bomberg

The first period of Hebrew book production in Venice, in which humanistic interest combined with more concrete economic concern, found its most illustrious promoter in the person of Daniel Bomberg (1483?-1553), a Christian from Antwerp who became known as "the Aldo (Manuzio) of Hebrew books". He left his native country with the intention of opening a printing shop in the city that was by then the centre of the international book market and, having obtained authorization from *La Serenissima* through the mediation of Brother Felice da Prato, a Jewish convert, and the favourable disposition of Pope Leo X towards Hebrew culture, he printed about two hundred works between 1516 and the middle of the century, availing himself of highly prestigious collaborators including Cornelio Adelkind, another converted Jew, Ya'aqobh ben Ḥayyim and, in the last phase of his activity, even the famous Elia Levita and some of the foremost typefounders of the period. His interest branched in many directions, from fundamental Hebrew texts and works of Midhrashic or Cabalistic character to grammars and prayer books for the various communities, but his fame rests above all on his editions of the *Bible* and the *Talmudh*. As for the former, after

the *Bibbia Rabbinica* of 1517 edited by Felice da Prato and dedicated to Pope Leo X, there appeared in 1524-25 a limited edition in four folio volumes containing, besides the Hebrew text, a translation in Aramaic and the most important commentaries, and edited, after lengthy research into the manuscripts and with deep philological dedication, by Ya'aqobh ben Ḥayyim; it was destined to remain a definitive reference work for centuries. A further edition in 1548 is of lesser value. His *Talmudh babilonese* appeared in 12 folio volumes between 1519 and 1523, edited by Cornelio Adelkind, while the 4 volumes of his *Talmudh palestinese* appeared in 1522-23. Bomberg sank his entire fortune in this worthy enterprise, but nevertheless, beset by disputes and competition, his activity began to go downhill towards the middle of the century. With ever more arduous financial setbacks, anti-Hebrew polemics kindled by Pope Paul III, and increasingly strict control of the press by the Reformers of the Padua Studio, he was obliged to abandon Venice, leaving the business in the hands of certain Venetian patricians whose interest was exclusively financial and who squabbled for supremacy in this very tricky commercial field.

נבואת

חזון

The *Bibbia Magna Rabbinica*, published in Venice by D. Bomberg in 1517: the *incipit* of the latter Prophets (Isaiah)

Venice, Lido Ancient Jewish Cemetery: Tombstone of Elia Levita, d. 5309 (1549)

Elia Levita was not only one of Bomberg's most celebrated colleagues during the latter years of his activity, but one of the best known personalities of Hebrew culture in the early 16th century. Born 'Eliyahu Halewi Baḥur in 1469, he left Germany to live in Mestre from 1492 to 1495, then in Padua until 1504, followed by Venice from 1509. He spent a decade in Rome teaching Hebrew to Cardinal Egidio da Viterbo, and when the city was sacked in 1527 he returned to Venice where, under the protection of Cardinal Grimani to whom he taught the "holy tongue" he worked on and off with Bomberg until the year before his death in 1549.

The career of Elia Levita is one of the best examples of Jewish influence on the outside world, above all in making known the language and culture of Judaism and creating a state of mutual respect and peaceful coexistence between the two worlds. He is known for works such as *The tradition of Tradition, The Book of Records*, and the translation into German-Jewish of the *Bovo d'Antona*, but his fame rests mainly on his celebrated grammar *Sepher ha-Baḥur* ("The Elect") of 1517, which formulated morphological and phonetic theses that caused a considerable stir among specialists, and offered clear articulation and straightforwardly laid down rules extremely valuable to any scholar with a personal interest in the holy tongue. His function was therefore as a mediator, publicizing precise "grammatical" structures traditionally regarded as arid, but in this specific case assuming a most substantial role. Not even his gravestone fails to point this out, describing him, amongst other things, as *medhaqdeq* (grammatical, precise).

39

Bomberg was briefly followed by Farri and Brucioli, but his most effective successor was a Venetian nobleman, Marco Antonio Giustiniani. From his printing press in Calle dei Cinque alla Giustizia Vecchia in Rialto, there flowed ninety editions within seven years (1545-52), all of exceptional quality, since Giustiniani was able to employ Bomberg's colleagues and use the characters made for him by the most famous type-founder of the period, the Frenchman Guillaume Le Bé, who happily landed in Venice in 1545; Giustiniani's work was however not without risks, for by now Hebrew book printing had acquired a purely commercial nature, nor without controversies at a time when ecclesiastical suspicion was mounting against the *Talmudh* (he printed an edition of eight hundred copies between 1546 and 1551), and competition was also on the increase. It was a repercussion from a controversy over the print-ing copyright of Maimonide's *Mishneh Torah* with typography by the rising Alvise Bragadin that put an end to his work. The two contenders appealed to the Inquisition, inadvertently providing it with a valid pretext for an offensive against the *Talmudh*, and this prompted Pope Julius III's bull of 1553 — which reached Venice in October of that year — ordering the destruction of many Hebrew books and the suspension of Jewish printing for about a decade.

In this context, the case of Me'ir Parenzo cannot but arouse interest. He was the only Jew who managed to print on his own account between 1545 and 1549, availing himself of typeface prepared for him by Le Bé. Building on his early experience as a proof reader, he published volumes on various subjects from Psalms and ritualistic works to scientific or literary texts, but his name is particularly linked with his edition of the *Mishnah* with commentary by the famous 'Obhadhyah da Bertinoro — now hard to find — which shows Jewish culture's constant concern with the fundamental works of its own ethical and religious tradition. Anyway, Me'ir Parenzo was not able to continue working for long. The mid-century crisis overwhelmed his initiative and obliged him to delay his typographical activity until later, when he became proof reader and contributor in the new enterprise of Alvise Bragadin.

Midhrash on the *Torah* and the Meghilloth, published in Venice by Marco Antonio Giustiniani in 5305 (1545)

Mishnayoth, order for *Neziqim* (Damages), with the commentary by 'Obhadhyah da Bertinoro, in the house of the patrician Carlo Querini (ed. 'Obhadhyah b. Zekharyah), printed by Me'ir b. Ja'aqobh Parenzo in Venice - 5309 (1549)

40

THE LEVANTINES IN THE OLD GHETTO

While the Ashkenazi intellectuals, in spite of segregation, were making their various contributions to the prestige of Venetian culture, something quietly happened in the spring and summer of 1541 that was destined to have decisive geographical, cultural and economic repercussions on the future life of the *Università degli ebrei.* In that year, the small but rich group of Levantine Jews who had been confined in the New Ghetto since the start of the century — though never explicitly mentioned in the documents — and were by now well aware of their importance to the Venetian economy, applied to the Senate for more suitable accommodation in the city, since the San Girolamo area was extremely restricted, already undeniably overcrowded, and therefore no longer adequate for the demands of all the commercial activity centering on the great trade with the east. Once again *La Serenissima*'s pragmatism prevailed over any other consideration. Venice was, in fact, going through another recession, mainly as a consequence of the 1537-40 war against the Turks; the volume of Levantine trade was gradually dwindling and the port of Ancona was offering increasing competition. The Levantines had been living for a long while in the great emporia of the eastern Mediterranean and had contact with all the major European ports; they were subjects of the Turkish empire and foreigners in Venice, so they doubtless appeared a reliable safety anchor to the eagerly calculating eyes of the *Cinque Savi alla Mercanzia*, the official body responsible for the sensitive mercantile sector. The Senate's reply to the "wayfarers" (as the Levantine Jews were still called) was therefore positive, allowing these "separate" Jews, subject to other regulations and restrictions, to carry on their work and store their merchandise in the area adjoining the Ghetto Nuovo, the Ghetto Vecchio, the long-abandoned foundry now occupied by a few houses and a good many gardens. They were to be answerable, although in a privileged way, to the *Cinque Savi*, who were careful not to compromise relations with such an important group. In 16th century history the decision marks a precise turning point in relations between Venice and the Jews. For one thing, the authorities endorsed the first considerable extension of the segregation area to include another part of the town very different in layout from the closed square of the Ghetto Nuovo. For another, it marks the beginnings of a different attitude on the part of the Republic towards one "nation" of the *Università* certainly more amenable and open-minded than it was towards the

41

Jewish woman and Jewish merchant from Turkey (16th C.)

Ashkenazim, an attitude that gave rise, in time, to serious friction and rivalry. Although they were both in the same situation and were able to present an internal unity and solidarity in moments of major threat, the Ashkenazim in the Ghetto Nuovo and the Sephardim in the Vecchio came, from that moment, to be two distinct entities as regards conditions, treatment and wealth; two groups sometimes opposed to each other, who only later, in times of common crisis, managed to find a more peaceful way of living together.

42

On 2 June 1541, having, at least two years previously, strategically abolished the import and export duties on many goods traded with the Near East, the Senate, recognizing that the greater volume of trade with Upper and Lower Rumania — the part of Europe at that time under Turkish domination and ruled from Costantinople — was currently in the hands of Levantine Jewish "wayfarers" agreed by a great majority to comply with the Jewish request to allow the rich merchants of the Ghetto to move into better accommodation in the Ghetto Vecchio, on condition that they accepted certain impositions: besides, obviously, the distinguishing sign, namely the yellow headgear, they insisted on temporary sojourn, limited to a maximum of four months (but later extended to two consecutive years), would not permit their families to stay with them, and forbade them to trade as pawnbrokers or rag-and-bone merchants, which was the exclusive domain of the German "nation".

In practice it was a commercial bargain, very different from the regulations under which the Germans and Italians were confined, but in continuing to insist on segregation, this time under the control of a different authority (*Cinque Savi alla Mercanzia* instead of the *Cattaver*), it effectively determined the

establishment of a Levantine "nation" a third ethnic group, distinct in customs and tradition from others in Venice's heterogeneous society. In this light, an attentive reading of historical documents presented by recent research (Ravid) refutes the practically canonic assertions put forward in the 18th century (Gallicciolli) and even taken up by more recent historians of the Venetian community (Roth, Milano etc), who saw the 1541 decree as the first confinement of the Levantine group within the walls of the Ghetto. Although the tone of the Senate's decree is conciliatory, the date only marks the widening of the confines of the already existing segregation, and a discrimination, in spite of all, that the later *condotta* of 1589 would officially recognize and legalize.

Decree to include the Ghetto Vecchio in the ghetto area for the benefit of the Levantine travellers (detail of an 18th C. print, the original in Venetian State Archives, *Senato, Mar.* reg. 26, 44v-44r, 2 June 1541)

"The Levantine Jews, who before the year 1541 vaguely formed an all embracing Nation, were in the said Year divided by Decree of the Excellent College into Wayfarers and Residents" (*Petition from the Levantines to his Serene Highness*, 22 March 1747). Thus a fairly late Jewish document, in some contrast to the dispositions in the decree of 2 June 1541, makes a distinction between "Wayfarers" and "Residents" with their families in the Ghetto within the Levantine group. This was a significant division that was in time to produce disturbing tension in the internal life of the entire group. The Levan-

Decreto dell' Eccell. Senato a favor Noftro.

1541. Adi 2. Giugno.

In Pregadi;

Ommiffis.

ET perchè la maggior parte delle Mercantie che vengono dalla Romania alta, & baffa per quanto fi vede, e conduta, & e in mano di Hebrei Mercadanti Levantini Viandanti li quali havendo repplicato alli Cinque Savj Noftri fopra la Mercantia, che non avendo loro da poter ftantiar in Ghetto per la ftretteza fua, ficcome per li prefatti Cinque Savj Noftri fopra la Mercantia e fta veduto li fia provifto di ftanzia per l' allozar; fuo però fia prefo acciochè habbino maggior caufa di venir con le Mercanzie fue in quefta Città a beneficio di quella, & haver loco dove allozar poffino ch' el fia per il Coll. dato liberta a quel Mag. li parerà, che debbano veder di accomodar detti Hebrei Mercanti Levantini Viandanti in Ghetto, & non li potendo allozar

tines were Jews from the west, ritualistically close to the Sephardim (from the Hebrew *sepharadi* meaning "Spanish") who, obliged to leave the Iberian peninsula during the dramatic expulsions of the late 15th century, had fled to the Middle East, mainly to the area occupied by the Turkish Empire, where they became subjects of the Grand Sultan and renewed their commercial activity, spreading out from great ports like Constantinople and Salonica to the busiest European markets until they accumulated vast riches and dominated the whole Balkan region. Doge Nicolò Contarini described them, not without distinct reservations, as "very astute people, explorers and bearers to the Turks of anything in their interests". Venice, however, regarded them with suspicion — there were some converts from Judaism among them (*marrani*) — but 43 welcomed them as indispensable factors in the State economy. From the first they displayed "oriental" fashions and habits, and kept them up for a long time, praying "in the Turkish manner" as Leon Modena attests, and showing off their opulence, not only in their imposing synagogue, but also in the style of both men's and women's dress. Speaking of the eastern Jews, Vecellio says, "And the men dress in the Syrian manner, in clothes like those of the Turks, except that on their heads they wear an eastern cap of yellowish voile, as the Levantine Jews in Venice still do". He describes the women as "Hebrews of Syria" and gives a picture of their clothes that certain Venetian-Jewish documents seem to show as in all respects similar (Boccato) to those of the Levantines living in the Ghetto: a tall, stiff cap on their heads, trimmed with stones and gilded rings, layers of gaudy skirts and bodice, under an exquisitely embroidered silken apron and a large shawl of fine linen, "footwear of coloured leather, as also Turkish slippers" and "around their necks . . . pearls of great price". These may, of course, be minor details, but are actually quite significant as ostentatious "signals" painfully underlining the difference in circumstance between them and the Ashkenazim confined in the Ghetto Nuovo.

The early Levantine settlement probably did not occupy the whole of the Ghetto Vecchio area lying between the Rio degli Agudi and the Rio di Cannaregio, but was mainly concentrated in the part nearest to the Campo di Ghetto Nuovo, running from the Agudi bridge — the only connection between the two areas of segregation — and the Campiello del Pozzo (later delle Scuole). Among many gardens there were a few houses, "old, ruined, and in poor condition" according to a document by the *Cinque Savi* dated 19 August 1541. They were mostly the property of the nobleman Leonardo Minoto and later his heirs who, prompted by the authorities, gave the current occupiers notice and leased the dwellings to the newcomers, from whom — since they were foreign residents, considered to all effect Turkish subjects — rents one third higher than before could be exacted (Carletto), as can be seen from letting agreements of 1604 and 1610. Although the old foundry area was not yet built up — as it would be later when a group from the west were also settled there — the *Cinque Savi* ordered it to be enclosed by a high wall all round the perimeter "to the mouth of the Campitello del Ghetto Vecchio from the side of the Cannaregio that runs towards the river, where the well stands" allowing only two gates at opposite sides. All windows facing outwards were bricked up, as were the doors of neighbouring Christian dwellings facing the Ghetto, while strict supervision was instituted under the control (only in this one matter) of the *Cattaver*.

In the light of such treatment, although the Levantines could consider themselves economically privileged compared with the Ashkenazim, their circumstances of segregation inside a compulsory enclosure seem to have been little different.

44

Venice - Calle di Ghetto Vecchio (formerly Strada Maestra)

THE "SCOLA LEVANTINA"

The concession for the Levantines to have fixed abode in the Ghetto Vecchio, although for limited periods and not yet officially sanctioned by a proper *condotta*, persuaded them to build their own synagogue, spacious and resplendent, near the centre of the new enclave. It seems that, through the architectural design and the impressive decorative features, they wished to proclaim the riches of their "nation" and their totally oriental taste for the grandiose and grandiloquent. The date of its construction, however, can be determined only approximately. "Divided since 1541 into wayfarers and residents," runs the already quoted petition of 1747, "all have erected their own Scola and adorned it with Silverware and Hangings serving the necessary and decorous exercise of the Ritual permitted them." It is indeed a case of fairly vague clues, and this text, equally lacking in precision, at least permits the date of the building's foundation to be corrected towards later years; a widespread oral tradition, not based on reliable documents, puts it at 1538, in effect anticipating the merchants' being allowed into the Ghetto Vecchio (Roth, Ottolenghi, Pinkerfeld, Sandri-Alazraki, etc.).

Erected, then, somewhere about the middle of the 16th century, the synagogue "which begins at the end of the Campiello del Pozzo as far as the end of the new Rosse factories" — to quote a building lease from the Minoto family of 5 February 1610 — became, from the moment the first stone was laid, the gathering point for community life for merchants passing through as well as for those already firmly settled in the Ghetto. Admittedly, no books or records have so far turned up, as they have for the Ashkenazi schools, that can throw light on the internal organization of the "sacred Levantine community" and its administration, but a "condition" agreed between wayfarers and residents on 17 May 1604 helps to clarify some important points. Since, in the latter part of the 16th century — the document suggests — internal friction and rivalry had arisen between the two Levantine groups to gain the administrative upper hand, they together arrived at a reciprocal understanding in order to avoid dangerous rifts, and this was to remain the basic convention to which they ad-

hered throughout the ensuing two centuries of the Ghetto's life. Having endorsed the terms of a stable reconciliation and fixed the letting conditions with the Minoto family, with a severe fine of five hundred ducats and excommunication for transgressors, the document goes on to state that all the synagogue's internal organizational and administrative structures should be upheld by twelve presiding custodians, six wayfarers and six residents, among whom the stewards were to be elected, while the other minor posts of sexton, secretary, scribe and cantor seem exactly the same as those of the other "nations". Only later, in 1617 and in the face of definitely extraordinary but established situations, was the number of stewards increased to thirteen, with a convention that an Italian or a German should be elected, provided he had "been making orisons" in the Scola for at least twenty five years, no less.

Anyway, the apparatus of internal administration is certainly not of paramount interest compared with such a monument. On the contrary, what counts most in this case is the building itself, the most imposing in the whole Ghetto, moreover the only one to stand alone and not be part of other buildings like the "scole" in the Ghetto Nuovo; it stands almost as a concrete symbol of its worshippers' increased state of security and in any case is the only one designed solely for prayer and study, by contrast with the multifunctionality typical of all the other synagogues, including the Spanish one, in the segregation area.

45

Venice - Museum of Jewish Art: a *parokheth* (drape for the Ark of the Covenant), a 19th C. copy of an older drape. In the medallion: "Gift of the Levantine Community in 5564 (1804)". Above: the Hebrew tents in the desert. Centre: the manna (*'omer lagulgoleth* - an omer a head - *Exodus* XVI, 16). Right, referring to the quails: *"Sha 'al wayyabhe' selayw welehem shamayim yasbi 'em — They asked, and he brought quails, And satisfied them with the bread of heaven "(Psalm CV, 40).* Left: *"Pathah tzur wayyazubhu mayim — He opened the rock, and waters gushed out" (Psalm CV, 41).*

The present synagogue, architecturally more mature and better proportioned than any other hall of worship in the Ghetto, only retains a minimal part of the original mid-16th century structure, but reflects, rather, an almost total adaptation to the fashions and stylistic accents of late 17th century Venice, particularly the dominant Longhenian atmosphere. Worshippers long uprooted from their own lands and having lived, for commercial reasons, in contact with many places, were clearly not able to preserve, alongside their standard ritual, a sound and unitarian artistic tradition, and therefore adopted for their own needs the architectural characteristics offered by local culture. Undeniable affinities with contemporary and slightly earlier Venetian buildings such as the Palazzo Flangini (Cassuto) unequivocally attest such an influence, which ultimately differentiates the Scola Levantina from the others, even in this respect. In their own schemes the other schools have always sought to keep alive traditional elements from their various countries of origin. This complete reliance on a taste extraneous to the Jewish world has brought other consequences, such as the complete absence of inscriptions — apart from the conventional Biblical exhortations — or of chronological pointers in plaques marking alterations or restorations, which might have helped to determine the stages in the building's history and its transformation over the centuries, as they do in the Ghetto Nuovo synagogue. Today's reconstruction of the building's evolution therefore relies exclusively on theories drawn from surviving archival documents, themselves fairly scarce.

For this reason it is impossible to be sure, first of all, about the finer features of the early synagogue. Its exact location is known, however, from the already quoted lease agreement of 1610, "at the end of the Campiello del Pozzo". Yet from a description, general though it is, in the "condition" of 1604, it appears that it was already an amply modulated and imposing two-storey structure, with an entrance hall on the ground floor, rooms for study and for meetings, the

main hall with the women's gallery on the first floor — possibly not too unlike the present one. The terms of the agreement between wayfarers and residents about their common use of the prayer hall speak, in fact, "of this Synagogue, as the Rooms below named Medras and Azarà, as also the Synagogue of the Women with the entrance and Stairs that ascend to the said Synagogue"; they also mention the decision that "all is to remain in the same way as it is presently found" unless the two parties should agree unanimously on the need for modifications; lastly they mention the silver, the hangings and the

precious materials that were kept there.

About a century later, however, this building was to prove inadequate or unsatisfactory, perhaps because of the "nation's" increased demands on it, perhaps because of a greater number of worshippers — documents of 1598 mention 51 resident heads of families, who were joined after that date by 64 more families, while the wayfarers numbered about a third of the brotherhood. A document of April 1680, after declaring that the stewards and the presidency of the Levantine congregation had ascertained that all the members "have deliberated concordantly to de-

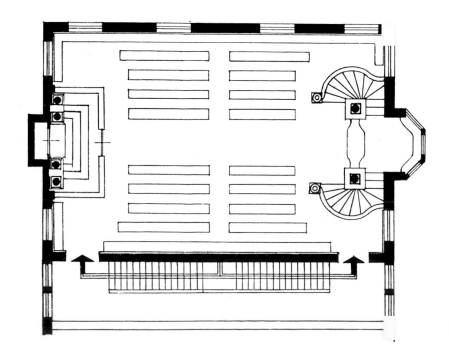

molish the School and rebuild it anew... demolishing it from the Foundations" and had undertaken the reconstruction of the building, states that "the Building having begun" the decision was taken, for reasons not specified, also "to extend the dimension of it" in other words enlarge it. The wayfarers contributed to the construction with "495 new-minted gold coins" while the residents relinquished some adjacent rooms to make way for the extension. It seems from the evidence that the undertaking was postponed at least until 1683, almost certainly for reasons of cost, but there is no doubt that by the early years of the 18th century the new synagogue must already have been completed, since a land register of 1713, preserved with the *Savi alle Decime* (Carletto), carries a description of a building that perfectly matches the configuration of the one that has survived to this day: "Scola

called Levantina for the use of Levantine Jewish wayfarers, with two doors on the ground floor and two large rooms on the ground floor, and above a great stone staircase there is the temple, and above another staircase there is a place that goes round half the said temple that serves for the women, where they say their prayers, with the casket of the Bible". The possibility of a dating on this evidence therefore becomes extremely important. It could in fact confirm certain theories not documentable until now, but put forward from several quarters for some time: firstly, the existence of Longhenian models, always assumed for stylistic reasons and never firmly confirmed; secondly, a possible participation by Brustolon (active during those very years in Venice, after his stay in Rome where he was familiar with Bernini's work) in the wooden decoration inside, always passed on by

oral tradition but never yet proved; lastly, these circumstances could justify the interruption of the perfect symmetry of the Campiello delle Scuole with reference to the central position of the well and the continuity of the decorative white line in the paving, inexplicable unless a later enlargement of the synagogue area is considered. Since then, slight interior alterations in the late 18th century, the instalment in 1836 of the Luzzatto *yeshibhah* in the hall on the ground floor of the Scola, and the successive touches of restoration in our own century do not seem to have substantially altered the structure of the building, while the recent total restoration in 1975 has attempted to return it to its early splendour. So it seems that the Levantine synagogue in its present shape can be attributed very closely to the 1680's. 47

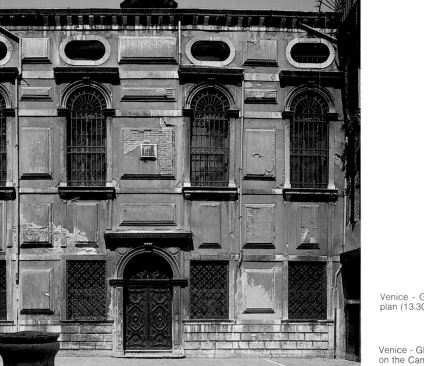

Venice - Ghetto Vecchio: Scola Levantina, Floor-plan (13.30m x 8.50m)

Venice - Ghetto Vecchio: Scola Levantina, Façade on the Campiello delle Scuole

The Levantine house of prayer is an independent building, even though attached to neighbouring dwellings. It has two façades, the main one on the Campiello delle Scuole and a side one on the Calle di Ghetto Vecchio, both of them with an entrance door, the first central, exactly opposite the internal staircase leading to the prayer hall, the second rather out of balance with the architectural rhythm. The main façade is in a commanding position, always visible to anyone coming into the Ghetto through the gateway from Cannaregio, and is a model of harmonious composition in which distant echoes of Longhena's "manner" can legitimately be identified. It has a high dado in rustic stonework, interrupted only by the wide entrance portal, similar to that of the Scola Spagnola, its wooden doors decorated with geometrical designs in high relief. Above that it is vertically divided into four by a row of square windows alternating with and surmounted by slightly protruding rectangles (of which the one on the extreme left has now been replaced with a plaque commemorating the Jewish dead of the First World War), then four wide, arched windows, topped by the same number of ovals, likewise interspersed by rectangles similar to those below. In the centre, a small white tablet bears the traditional inscription "*Zekher laḥurban — In memory of the destruction of the Temple*".

The side face, although repeating the compositional scheme of the main façade, is different in a special way, for between the two large, arched windows is a structure characteristic of other synagogues in the Ghetto, consisting here of a semi-hexagonal crescent with a wide window each side and surmounted by a shell shaped hood; it is the protrusion of the *bimah* in which, more than elsewhere, can be recognized the repetition of the architectural *liagó* (sun balcony) motif so common in Venetian palaces.

Presenting a really difficult puzzle in this section on the Calle del Ghetto Vecchio is the existence of a second entrance door, in a position hardly associated with any other structural feature. The doorway on the Campiello, in fact, is exactly opposite the central staircase, which then divides, with deliberately theatrical effect, in a similar way to the one in the Scola Spagnola, and leads to two entrances to the hall of worship. But this second doorway obliges the visitor to follow an unnatural path on his way to the hall of worship, creating a certain perplexity as to its legitimate justification. The most common opinion held by scholars is that in its original design the present synagogue had only the main entrance and that the second one had to be added later — with little aesthetic sense — in the 19th century, when the Scola Luzzatto, from the Ghetto Nuovo, was installed in a specially made side section of the vestibule, although the previously cited land register of 1713 seems to point firmly to the contrary. It speaks explicitly of "two doors on the ground floor" and of "two large rooms on the ground floor" existing since the edifice was rebuilt in the late 17th century, while actually listing the synagogue in the row of buildings on the *Strada Maestra*, not in the Campiello. This leads one to suppose that the so-called second entrance was really the one effectively used from the beginning. Is it possible to imagine that demands of space, orientation, and adaptation to buildings already there, plus the desire to enlarge the synagogue, perhaps giving it a façade to rival the nearby Scola Spagnola, all combined to influence the builders to produce a design that turned out very successful on the Campiello, and practical, but rather insensitive from the asthetic point of view, on the Calle? Until fresh clues are discovered, this seems to be the only possible supposition.

The ground floor is therefore divided into two rooms. The one on the south side may originally have been devised as a study area, but has been occupied since 1836 by the interior furnishings of the Scola Luzzatto, reconstructed there. The other one functions as the actual vestibule; it is a vast rectangular space, with the characteristic benches round the walls, adorned with a fine ceiling. Immediately to the right of the entrance is an ancient tablet, now barely legible, reminding the faithful that humility and charity win their reward in heaven. Beyond, there is a box marked "Gift of the Company of Piety and Charity" an alms box belonging to the "*Industria de la Casseta del K.K. delli Signori Levantini*" and the plaque marking the visit to Venice of Sir Moses Montefiore in 1875. On the opposite side is a washbasin, a collection box for funds for the land of Israel, and then the first stairs leading up to the hall of worship. After the first flight there is an inscription exhorting people to faith and prayer (the Hebrew part uses an acrostic with the name of God) similar to that in the Scola Italiana: "*Humble in act . . .*". Two more flights, facing each other and built perhaps in imitation of the nearby Scola Spagnola or else as a practical solution to the need for access to the hall of worship, pass various service rooms and lead finally to two entrances to the prayer hall.

The overwhelming characteristic of the prayer hall itself is a disproportionate degree of decoration for the limited space available. Nevertheless the designer of the entire ensemble, though yielding to late baroque taste, must be admired for having managed to create a sufficiently unified and composed setting for prayer and contemplation. Forbidden, as is well known, to use statues or images, he has resorted to a large number of chandeliers and candlesticks to fill the space, particularly around the Ark of the Covenant, and the skilful introduction of colour in his choice of large wall panels of damask cloth, which blend perfectly with the sombre colouring of the impressive wooden *bimah* and the massive ceiling decoration, thus achieving a balanced interior worthily representative of Levantine sensitivity. Apart from this dominant feature, the hall offers no outstanding detail. It is, in fact, on the normal rectangular plan, with the twin focal points of the *'aron* and the *bimah* facing each other on the short sides, connected by the typical benches running along the wood-panelled walls and the pews for the worshippers lying parallel to the long sides, leaving the usual space in the middle. The women's gallery itself, cleverly camouflaged behind heavy gratings on the entrance side that balance the symmetrical oval openings on the opposite wall, echoes the schemes in the Scola Canton and the Scola Italiana, though in a more markedly ornamental way. Next to the two focal points, the wall and ceiling decoration is most impressive; the walls are covered with wooden mouldings and damask panels, between the windows too, while the ceiling is closely linked to the stylistic character of the majestic *bimah*,

decorated with geometric wooden carvings and gilding of late baroque style. The two entrance doors are 18th century (the one by the *bimah* bears the date 5546-1786), and very elaborate in the marble panels that surmount them. Their off-centre positions on a long wall and near to the hall's two focal points are obviously determined by the positions of the access stairs. Although fitting handsomely into the scheme, they add little, except that above carvings worked in two colours they do present some of the few inscriptions that exist in the synagogue. On the arch of the one by the *'aron* is the verse about Jacob's dream: "*Mah-nno-ra'hammaqom hazzeh, 'eyn zeh ki 'im-*

beyth 'elohiym — How dreadful is this place! This is none other but the house of God" (*Genesis* XXVIII, 17), and higher up, in the small oval near the women's gallery: "*Bekha'A. hasithi — In Thee, oh Lord, have I trusted*" (*Psalm XXXI, 2)*, while the one near the *bimah* has two verses: "*Pithhu-li sha'arey - tzedheq 'abho'bham 'odheh yah — Open to me the gates of righteousness; I will enter into them, I will give thanks unto the Lord*" (*Psalm* CXVIII, 19), and "*Zeh-hashsha 'ar la 'A. tzaddiqim ya-bho'u bho — This is the gate of the Lord; the righteous shall enter into it*" (*Psalm* CXVIII, 20). The oval below the women's gallery bears the same date as the door, 1786.

Venice - Ghetto Vecchio: Scola Levantina (section)

49

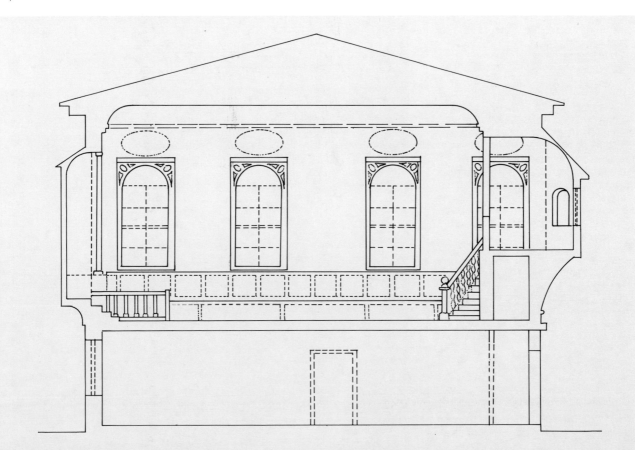

Attention, however, is once again wholly concentrated on the hall's two focal points. Arguably the less effective of the two is the 'aron, fascinating and impressive, but rather compressed inside too restricted a space. It was obviously built with the one in the nearby Scola Spagnola in mind; the doors to the Ark of the Covenant are engraved with the Ten Commandments and the date 5542 (1782) and framed by a complex structure, a wide arch over a sort of niche formed by four striated Corinthian columns resting on tall plinths, preceded by four steps and crowned by a tympanum. It is certainly not an exceptional design, but in this case lack of originality is compensated for by the multi-coloured marbles with a general tone that blends wonderfully with the austere colours of the surround-

50   ings, and throws into greater relief the two inscriptions on contrasting coloured sections above the whole. The first, on a black background, says " *'Eshta-ḥaweh 'elheykhal qodhshekha we 'o-dheh 'eth shemekha — I will worship toward thy holy temple and give thanks unto thy name*" (*Psalm* CXXXVIII, 2). The second, on a gold ground, repeats the Talmudh, *Berakhoth*, 28 b: "*Da' li-phney mi 'atah 'omedh — Think before Whom thou standest*" which can also be read in the Scola Spagnola. The most distinctive feature is a fine marble balustrade with multi-coloured columns and insets, which stands around and in front of the whole feature, creating for it a separate space ornamented with beautifully worked candelabra and candlesticks. In the centre, a small brass railing of the 18th century style bears the inscription "*Gift of the belov-ed R. Menaḥem b. Maimon Vivante to God in the year 5546 (1786) ['odhekha beysher lebhabh — I will give thanks unto thee with uprightness of heart* (*Psalm* CXIX, 7)]*".

Venice - Ghetto Vecchio: Scola Levantina, the 'aron

Venice - Ghetto Vecchio: Scola Levantina, ceiling

Venice - Ghetto Vecchio: Scola Levantina, the ▸ bimah

While the impact of the *'aron* depends largely on the subtle handling of colour, the dominant qualities of the *bimah* facing it are without doubt its imposing severity and its skilful wood carving, which strongly suggests the hand of Andrea Brustolon, supporting the oral tradition that he worked on the Scola Levantina.

Echoes recent and remote must surely have contributed to the original design and realization of the structure, from a hint of Bernini's canopy in St Peter's (which Brustolon admired when he was in Rome) to a suggestion of the nearby altar in the Chiesa degli Scalzi, combined with the memory of the ancient columns of Solomon's Temple. But a typically 17th century taste for the theatrical has been imposed on all these influences, responding completely to the characteristic Levantine tendency towards oriental magnificence. The *bimah* rests on a high base decorated with geometrical and floral motifs and encircled by two wide, curving staircases of twelve steps with beautifully shaped banisters. The *bimah* itself is framed by two great twisted columns, intricately carved, and an austere architrave which links directly with the ceiling cornice, suggesting an intimate decorative unity governed by the same taste and style. The grand, majestic effect is further enhanced by the semi-hexagonal apse in the background (the protruding crescent on the short wall outside), set with a wide, arched window at each side and an umbrella vault, its six segments richly inlaid with repeated geometric relief motifs. In all, the creators of the place from which men pray and read out the word of the Torah determined to make it into the true hub of the hall. One might object that the structure is too massive in relation to the size of the hall, or that the ornamental scheme is too ostentatious, but no one could deny that the Levantines effectively succeeded in endowing their synagogue with the most unusual and striking *bimah* of all the "Scole" in Venice.

HARD TIMES

It is a common phenomenon throughout the history of the Diaspora that all periods of social, economic or political difficulty have worked to the disadvantage of the Jewish population. For the Ghetto on the Venetian Lagoon, the three troubled decades in the middle of the 16th century were sad evidence of this. For one thing, Venice was squeezed between the expansion of Turkish power in the Mediterranean and Spanish power in Italy. For another, it could not escape the spreading spirit of the Counter Reformation, and was powerless to avert consequent fits of anti-Semitism which had a dire effect on the situation within the area of confinement around San Girolamo. The "nation" hardest hit was, naturally, that of the Ashkenazim, until that time the Hebrew *Università's* only official representative to the authorities. The settlement of the Levantines in a decidedly privileged position in the Ghetto Vecchio had already begun to generate some ill feeling destined to increase over the years, but judged from an objective point of view the main distress occurred in the moneylending field. Continual difficulties were encountered in running the banks following the increase in tax pressure and the lowering of the interest rate — it had dropped to 12% between 1548, when the *condotta* was renewed at the price of increased taxes and the dire ban on book publishing, and 1558 when new, harsher regulations were brought into force by the *Sopraconsoli*; this moved the Senate, after long discussions in 1565, to renew the next *condotta* with a clause making the entire community, no longer individual operators, responsible for the election of individual bankers and therefore, indirectly, for the handling of affairs in any case of bankruptcy. This had serious consequences for the whole community. In the Venetian pawnbroking sector it caused a radical upset; the later imposed reduction of the interest rate to 10% initiated, as explicitly declared in that *condotta*, the future recognition of the Jewish banks as the "poverty banks" meaning that from then on they would assume the social function elsewhere performed by the

Monti di Pietà. Nor did the Jews, for their part, produce any reactions capable of warding off a scheme that would later rebound damagingly on other mainland communities called in to subsidize the Ghetto Nuovo credit market.

The critical downward trend, however, was to be accelerated by other events at that time, of varying importance but all bringing dire consequences. One was the enforcement in Venetian territory of Pope Julius III's decree against the *Talmudh*, in which the public bonfires of Hebrew books caused grave damage to their culture and produced a ten-year standstill in Hebrew

printing (1553-63). Other episodes, apparently marginal, but destined to have a deep effect on the conditions of the entire community, were the renewal in 1550 of the edict expelling converts from Judaism (*marrani*) from the Veneto region, and the perpetual banishment inflicted on the celebrated Joseph Nassi — Giovanni Miches — in 1553, for having extracted an enormous dowry from La Serenissima by abducting and then marrying his cousin Beatrice Mendes (but repealed in 1567 after Nassi, who was Duke of Naxos and other Cyclades Islands, had become a leading personage at the court of Selim II).

The time of greatest tension, however, was during the 1570's, particularly after the Battle of Lepanto in 1571. This victory over the Turks was, in fact, to have a bad repercussion on the Jewish "infidels" whom some people actually blamed for the war because of a plot hatched by Nassi. A decree of expulsion was issued in terms more harsh and peremptory than ever before, leaving little room for hope and ending in the suspension of all activity for practically a year. It was a very threatening period, and the Ashkenazim survived only by making costly concessions that placed them in a position of total dependence on the whims of the State. Another influential Jew, Salomone Ashkenazi, native of Veneto but risen to prominent rank at the Ottoman court, succeeded in modifying the anti-Jewish atmosphere in gratitude for his role in the peace talks between Venice and the East, but in any case the current economic situation itself made it obvious that if the Jews left, the age-old problem of the Monti di Pietà would return (Ravid). This led the *Avogadori* Priuli and Gritti to intercede for the withdrawal of the drastic decree, which was effected after three successive votes in the Senate, but on conditions that considerably worsened the state of the Ghetto inhabitants. The measures brought in with the final decision in 1573 were the imposition of further additional taxes and the definitive transformation of the pawn shops into veritable public assistance offices. The Venetian *Università* and some banks on the mainland committed themselves to invest a further 50.000 ducats permanently locked up in the running of the moneylending market at a reduced interest rate of 5% per annum. From the date the decree of expulsion was withdrawn the banks became officially recognized for all time, like the corresponding humanitarian institute of the Grey Friars in Venice, which was needed by a large part of the Venetian population. They had by now become *de facto* what Simone Luzzatto was to call "poverty banks" and were to be an ever heavier burden on the German "nation" and increasingly hard to maintain. By the end of the century they had been reduced to three, called by the colours of their respective receipts, black, red and green, and they began to draw an overwhelming number of customers attracted by the favourable lending conditions, which put them in an extremely precarious position and obliged them to deposit an exorbitant amount of backup funds. Historians agree that until there were official interventions to block and restore the situation in the early 17th century, this was the most tense and anxious period the Ashkenazim suffered, and this radical transformation in the running of their banks was the highest price they had to pay for their stable residence in the Ghetto Nuovo.

53

A banker at his bench (from G. Grevembroch, *Gli abiti de'veneziani*)

Venice - Academy. Paolo Veronese, *The Battle of Lepanto* (detail)

The restrictive pressure from the outside world in the late 16th century was immediately reflected culturally inside the Ghetto, where the spirit of the Counter Reformation led to attitudes markedly different from the previous humanistic Renaissance ones.

The Levantines brought with them a culture more inclined towards a pluralistic view of the various trends within Judaism, and their arrival had without doubt encouraged Venetian Jews to be more open-minded, alongside traditional Talmudism, towards aspects of mysticism until now looked at only in an elitist way or for the sake of intellectual curiosity. The distribution of the *Qabbalah* and its translation among the general public, often allied, in the practice of daily worship, with the dominant Halakhic attitude (Bonfil), soon acquired a "conservative" reputation, however. Without undervaluing the traditionally easy relations with Venetian intellectuals, each cultural commitment seems, in fact, to have been more emphatically inward-looking, a defensive response to outside anti-Jewish severity, in their all-out quest for their own identity and their own historical personality, so that a heritage of ethical and spiritual values should not be irrevocably lost. Notwithstanding the strict controls and prohibitions imposed by *La Serenissima*, it was in a sense this response that ultimately favoured the revival of the Hebrew press, which in 1563 resumed its successful development, albeit within precise limits. Noble Venetian families such as Bragadin and Di Gara, no longer with the pioneering humanistic spirit that had animated Bomberg, but with purely commercial intentions, making the most of previous experiences and often employing printers and proof readers of proven ability, took up an activity that was to continue in Venice for centuries, even in competition with the Hebrew printing shops of Amsterdam and eastern Europe.

Alvise Bragadin, founder of the well-known "Bragadina Press" which was active until the mid 18th century, having started production in 1550 with the famous edition of the *Mishneh Torah* by Maimonide that caused the fatal dispute with Giustiniani, went back to work in 1563 after the "black decade". Amongst the works he published under the signature of Parenzo to avoid using his own name was the famous *Shulḥan 'arukh* (Prepared Table) — on request from the author himself, Joseph Karo (1564) —, the large encyclopaedia of ritual, which represents perhaps the greatest compendium of Sephardic spiritual matters, destined to become one of the fundamental texts of Hebrew culture. Without achieving results of high value, but always dignified even in the face of considerable difficulties and restrictions, Bragadin retired in 1575, leaving his business in the hands of his son Giovanni, who kept it going, with equal dedication, for a number more years.

Joseph Karo, *Shulḥan 'arukh*, signed by Me'ir b. Ya'aqobh Parenzo for Alvise Bragadin, printed in Venice for the first time in 1564-65

54

פירוש התורה

מהחכם השלם דון יצחק אברבנאל זצל

ידד כמטר על גזלהזמיח ציצים ופרחים בחמשה חומשי תורה
ויצא ונלחם עם כל אשר לא יעלה על שמים שיאה
גם פריו יתן בעתורלהבין ולהשביל
בה דבר אמת לאמתו

וחוגה בעין רב על ידי החכם כמהרר שמואל ארקוולטי יצו

מדפס כמצות השר מסיר זואן כרלבדין כן סורין מסיר אלווזי כלאבדין

על ידי נאן כויס כלר לפר פרינצו יצו

בונינציאה

בשנת השלט לבריאת עולם

Pirush hattorah by Don Yitzḥaq Abrabanel, printed
by Giovanni di Alvise Bragadin, edited by Samuele
Archivolti, cur. 'Asher Parenzo, Venice 1579

Giovanni Bragadin's production was fairly scant, only about fifteen editions, and limited to the reprinting of already familiar works or the reissue of illustrious texts with new layouts. This is a sign of the difficult conditions under which he managed to operate the Hebrew press in those restless years of the late 16th century. The 1571 ban on Hebrew book printing and the harsh control of the *Esecutori contro la Bestemmia* always reluctant to grant licences and severe in their censure, demonstrate how much more intransigent *La Serenissima* had become in this sector too. The seizure and destruction of about 8.000 books in 1568 had brought upon the Jews themselves and on the commercial operators a disaster in the order of 18.000 ducats (Grendler). The Holy See twice proceeded against Marc'Antonio Giustiniani — already forced to suspend work at the time the *Talmudh* was destroyed —, accusing him, wrongly, of having illegally printed Hebrew texts, and against his son Antonio, strongly suspected of illegal trade in Hebrew publications, thus eliminating from the printing scene a family whose work had been particularly distinguished.

Bragadin should be equally admired for his courage, in spite of his evident limitations and his less than brilliant philological accuracy. The *Pirush hattorah* by the famous Don Yitzḥaq Abrabanel remains one of his most important undertakings. Just as admirable in such a climate are the other publishers who at that time trod with courage the difficult path of Hebrew publishing: Zanetti, Cavalli, Grifio and, above all, Giovanni Di Gara — perhaps the most deserving to carry the title of Bomberg's heir — whose work continued into the next century. Except for the last, they were all minor publishers, their work more susceptible to the whims of the authorities, whose interference around 1568 considerably reduced their activity, but together they represent a significant presence on the late 16th century book scene. At the turn of the century, the Zanetti brothers managed to print nearly thirty volumes, albeit not of great worth. Before the 1568 crisis Giorgio Cavalli printed about fifteen, while Giovanni Grifio published at least five, and this is no small achievement in such hard times.

55

In this difficult climate, the wide-spread atmosphere of hostility finally touched such representatives of the "Hebrew nation" as doctors who, though shut in the Ghetto and obliged to wear a distinguishing sign, had hitherto enjoyed privileged treatment. They were welcomed for their scientific knowledge and their access to publications inaccessible to the western world, allowed to study for a degree (received from the Counts Palatine) at Padua, rewarded by a sort of probation, with permission to leave the Ghetto even at night for visits or scientific meetings — though these had to be recorded — and in spite of the fact that, under their prevailing system of treatment, therapy coincided to a great extent with religious ritual centred on binomial confession and communion (Vanzan), they had always found in practice that they were judged and given rights as doctors who treat and cure, rather than discriminated against as infidel Jews who treat the body but damn the soul.

Nevertheless, the bulls of Pope Paul V of the Carafa (1555) and Pope Pious V of the Medici (1564) had forbidden Christians to consult Jewish doctors and introduced the so-called *professio fidei* as a preliminary ritual to taking a degree, and now this spirit of Counter Reformation began to make its repressive effect felt as far away as Venice. In 1567, in spite of the objections expressed by Paduan intellectuals, the *Collegio Medico-fisico* (College of Doctors-Physicians) to *La Serenissima* was powerless to resist striking its Jewish members off the register, furthermore forbidding the circulation of medical research findings outside the restricted circle of enrolled members. Yet on many occasions, during epidemics or plagues, Jewish doctors had spent and were spending their efforts, regardless of risk, on behalf of the citizens, in close collaboration with the *Provveditori alla Sanità* (Health Superintendents). This lent added vehemence to the protest of one of the most noted doctors of the time, Dawidh de' Pomis, who had sought refuge on the Lagoon after leaving papal territory, and had found the atmosphere in Venice more permissive

than elsewhere. He was an illustrious scientist and linguist, author of works of a technical nature, also of a famous panegyric to the origins of Venice. In his best-known work, *De Medico hebreo enarratio apologetica* (1588), he set out to defend the Jewish doctor's work and selflessness, above any suspicion, putting the patient before any social or religious consideration, and claiming, against all impositions, the freedom to practise a skill which, beyond faith or profession, cannot but ennoble all mankind: "... a doctor, as a doctor and as a Jew, follower of the divine law of Moses, cannot commit reprehensible acts, as experience has many times demonstrated, since the Jew considers the Christian not as a personal enemy ... but as a brother". The response to the great scientist's high intentions was not slow in coming; the protection of illuminated minds, such as Cardinal Grimani, or the favours granted to the most famous doctors, cited as examples by de' Pomis himself, were in effect the just recognition of work that truly "gloriam Judaeis auxit ... per totum orbem" (increases the reputation of Jews in all the world).

Jewish doctor

Cambridge University Library: Veneto Jewish doctor (15th C.) with medicinal herbs (Ms. Dd 10.68, f. 37v.)

Maḥazor of the Italian ritual (Soncino, 1485), Form ▶ of prayer for feastdays

THE "SCOLA ITALIANA"

The drastic events of 1571-73 were a decided setback in the conditions of Venetian Jews, but afterwards the Ghetto seems to have made a real recovery in both its social life and its buildings, bringing the Jewish quarter to fully integrated maturity. An early and fairly significant symptom of a new cultural and religious atmosphere was the building, almost fifty years after the German synagogue, of the *Scola Italiana*, finished in 5335 (1575) according to the inscription on a shield on the façade over the *campo*. The hall is certainly less harmonious than the sophisticated Scola Canton, less rich and imposing than the Scola Grande Tedesca, but no less austere in its strict colour scheme, nor lacking in origianl luminous effects which create an impression of space and airy composure. The "Italian" Jews in the Ghetto built it as a place to celebrate their own ritual, where the singing sounded "more pure and restful" according to the testimony of Leon Modena. They were a minority group, not cconomically privileged, never to form an independent "nation" and always lumped together with the Germans, but at the same time, from the qualitative, cultural and religious point of view, a group in no way inferior to other ethnic bodies living in the segregated quarter. Most of these members of the "Sacred Italian Community" had come from the centre and south of Italy during the late medieval stream of migration, bringing a culture based on the philosophical and theological tendencies that had characterized the "Scuola Romana". They had been able to integrate well enough with the prevalently "Talmudic" principles of the Ashkenazim, giving rise to a rich and varied intellectual attitude interwoven with many strands that succeeded, in an overall positive eclecticism, in modifying both the intransigent severity and general narrow-mindedness of certain Germans and the equally general open-mindedness of their original group towards outside attitudes. In the seventies, in fact, the atmosphere being receptive, their "scola" was the source of a new rush towards the *Qabbalah*. This spreading interest was aroused by the lessons of the young Rabbi Menaḥem A. da Fano, and was destined not only to crystallize into precise modifications to the text of the daily ritual (Bonfil), but primarily to be translated, also within devotional practice, into the creation of many *Confraternite pie*, characteristic of Ghetto life, which condensed the philanthropic and social efforts of various Jewish groups (Horowitz).

Although obliged to live under economic conditions that afforded little working scope to small money-lenders or those reduced to the rag-and-bone trade, typical of all Italian ghettos, they managed to organize themselves around their own *Beyth Keneseth*, remembering the Roman tradition, with their own rabbis and their own functionaries in a hierarchical structure that was able to ensure their own autonomy while still respecting the demands of the entire *Università*. The surviving *Regolamenti* of 1644 (Pacifici) outline an organization very similar to that of the Scola Grande Tedesca, with a *Wa'adh*, the general assembly, consisting of all those who had attended the Scola for at least ten years — some seats were hereditary — who elected three *parnasim*, wardens responsible for management and administration, backed up by a *hazzan*, the officiant, preacher and rabbi, and a *shammash*, the secretary cum sexton, with two *gabbayim*, managers, and a *gizbar*, or treasurer, to attend to their strict orders. Alongside this perfectly functioning administrative system and completing the efficient working structure, certain surviving registers give a glimpse of a noticeable emphasis on philanthropic and humanitarian work, both at home and abroad; their especial secular commitment to the

יהא אדם ירא שמים בסתר ומודה על האמת ודובר אמת בלבבו וישכים ויאמר רבון כל
העולמים לא על צדקותינו אנחנו מפילים תחנונינו לפניך כי על רחמיך הרבים מה אנו מה
חיינו מה חסדנו מה צדקתנו מה כחנו מה גבורתנו מה נאמר לפניך יי אלהינו ואלהי אבותינו הלא
הגבור סאין לנגדך ואנשי השם כלא היו וחכמים כבלי מדע ונבנים כבלי השכל הדא כל ימי
תדו ובדו רמי חיינו הבל לפניך שכן כתוב בדברי קדשך ובותר האדם מן הבהמה וגו כי ה
הכל הבל ... אבל אנחנו עמך בני בריתך בני אברהם אוהבך שנשבעת לו בהר המוריה
זרע יצחק יחידך שנעקד על גבי המזבח עדת יעקב בנך בכורך שמאהבתך שאהבת אותו
ומשמחתך ששמחת בו קראת אתי ישראל וישרון ... לפיכך אנו חייבים להודות ... ו ה
ולשבחך לפארך ...

אתה הוא עד שלא נברא העולם ואתה הוא משנברא העולם
אתה הוא בעולם הזה ואתה הוא לעולם הבא קדש את שמך על מקדישי שמך שנק קדש את
שמך בעולמך ובישועתך תרים ותגביה קרננו ברוך מקדש שמו ברבים

good of the Jewish community in the Holy Land, Safed in particular (Carpi), from the 16th to the 18th century, is without doubt one of the characteristic traits that demonstrates their determination to keep alive their ties with the land of their forefathers. The Italians, therefore, were not a minor presence, as some would have it, nor a group of secondary importance, but a community capable of producing men and institutions of prestige, on a par with those produced by other, more famous, "nations" of the Ghetto.

The desire to keep alive an additional idealistic link with the country of their diasporic residence also informs the structure and decoration of the "Italian" Jews' synagogue. It is distinguished by an architectural design that quite clearly reveals a harmonious integration between locally available models and distant echoes of Rome that characterize certain synagogues in the ghetto on the Tiber. Their evolution over the years was slow, but its path is sufficiently clear from documents and inscriptions.

The hall completed in 5335 (1575) on the top floor of a building rented for worship from "the Magnificent Signor Bernardo Bruolo" was almost certainly not the first to have been frequented by the "Sacred Italian Community". Plaster has fallen from the walls, revealing the existence on the first floor of five windows, two of which have been bricked up, prompting the supposition (Cassuto) that from the time they were confined in the Ghetto until the 1570's the Italians made use of a primitive synagogue, not otherwise identifiable, on the floor that is actually punctuated by the five windows, reached from the entrance still recognizable today, on the left, through a modest doorway.

Only later did the stabilization of the social situation after 1571 and the consequent population increase lead to the creation of the larger, identifiable hall of worship, between the existing buildings, using the typical motif of the windows

onto the *campo* and the graceful little umbrella cupola rising over the luminous apse beneath. The text of the Scola's "*Instrumento di affittanza*" drawn up on 27 November 1609 between the widow Signora Giustina Bruolo and the *parnasim* Abramo Mortaira and Lion Luzzatto, reveals the information that the prayer hall, of bifocal, irregular rectangular plan, with an entrance at right angles to both the *'aron* and the *bimah*, as in the nearby Scola Canton, was preceded by a vestibule, whose purpose was indeed one of "passage" between the hall itself and the stairs which climbed rather tortuously from a renovated entrance on the ground floor, and between the stairs and the rooms occupied as dwellings by certain brothers Saraval, on one side, and Calimani, on the other. Besides this, the new entrance from the campo was emphasized by a portico structure, later (19th century?) surmounted by a another,

temple-like, structure with a tympanum — a distant echo of similar Roman designs — which was also intended, however, to signal the presence of one of the Ghetto's pawnbrokers. The women's gallery was sited "in a place upstairs for the Women" in a "withdrawing room" probably next to the *bimah* itself. Since, nevertheless, "the opposite wall and likewise the roof threatens to collapse" as the contract says, the landlady that year gave the synagogue administrators permission to raise the walls on all sides of the hall and the vestibule and to make a new roof, with freedom to open "a window overlooking the Canal, being allowed also, when making the said roof, to reduce the

Venice - Ghetto Nuovo: Scola Italiana, floorplan (app. 10m x 9.30m)

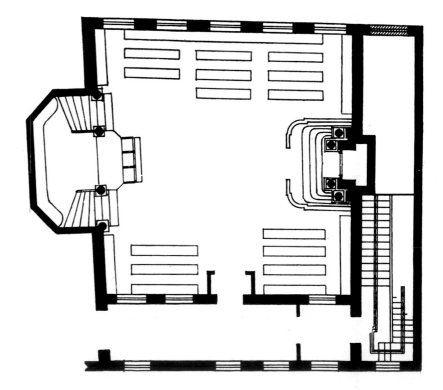

place for the women over the above-mentioned passage" and "make the windows between this" and the hall itself. It is as yet impossible to know exactly when the restoration was carried out, with the permitted transformations, because there is nothing about it in the text of the regulations or the various surviving *pinqasim*, or registers.

One certainly cannot believe that they managed to wait until late 5499 (1739-40), the era of Rabbi Isacco Pacifico and the superintendents Kohen, Nizza and Osimo, who "conducted" the synagogue's great renovation, described in a long inscription that can be read in the vestibule. That date, which saw important renovations in all the Venetian synagogues, more likely refers to the complete assemblage of the *bimah* (later restored), the ceiling decoration, and probably the *'aron*, but within already defined architectural structures, together with the decorative scheme on the lower part of the walls, all features that do not seem to have subsequently undergone more than superficial modifications.

The latest conspicuous work in the prayer hall in the early 19th century (5570 - 1810), also aimed at "matching with magnificence" the wall coverings, as indicated by the Hebrew inscription posted above the entrance door to the hall, without significantly affecting the importance of the walls themselves. According to the acrostic of the said inscription, it was done by one Isacco Norza, probably to honour the memory of his father Abramo; in addition, he had celebratory epigraphs placed along the entire upper section of the walls, also with an eye to their colour effects. No crucial alterations were produced by the restoration of the *bimah* in 5569 (1809), according to the indication affixed below it, nor by the early 19th century decoration of the *'aron*, or the wooden balustrade round the Ark of the Covenant, added in 5602 (1842). The overall style of the walls has remained 17th century, and that of the decorations, 18th century. Only the renovation of the stairs, begun — according to an "*Instrumento*" signed in 1803 with the "brothers Muchiachion" — by returning the entrance from the *campo* to its original design, produced an appreciable change inside the building, although not in the prayer hall, bringing the entire complex to its present form. For this reason, the cleaning and restoration begun in 1985, after the questionable interventions of 1970, have aimed completely at restoring the authentic appearance of the original design.

59

Old print of the Roman "Scole"

Like the other synagogues in the Ghetto Nuovo, the Scola Italiana would blend into the other buildings on the south side of the *campo* were its presence not indicated by certain particularly significant external structures. Unquestionably the most striking is the portico, formed by two columns and two Doric pilasters supporting a straight cornice. This is surmounted by a temple-like structure, classical in style, with a tympanum of later origin, possibly 19th century, hemmed at the sides by a simple balustrade, the left-hand pillar of which is topped with the small figure of a lion. There are admittedly no original or distinctive features. This portico functioned as the entrance to the synagogue built in 1575, and also marked the location of one of the Ghetto's pawnbrokers. It demonstrates the most direct influence of Roman design on architectural schemes by Jews who had emigrated to Venice, as do the outside of the Scola Catalana and the *'aron* of the Italian Temple. Alongside this unusual feature, on the first floor, is a row of windows, two of them bricked up, recording the existence of an early synagogue, reached through the small entrance on the left and frequented by the Italian Community during the first seventy years of their segregation in the Ghetto, until it was replaced by the larger synagogue erected on the floor above. This can be identified from outside by the traditional five-window motif and a small, baroque, umbrella-shaped cupola in white stone on the west wall, poised on a high octagonal tambour with large windows that let light through the wide lantern onto the *bimah* below. A small shield above the centre window bears the legend "Sacred Italian Community" and the date 5335 (1575), while a square tablet below the same window is set up to recall the destruction of the Temple. The sign "Sacred Italian Community" is repeated near the small entrance doorway which revives the early access to the synagogue, admitting to a small, dark vestibule from where a steep staircase leads to the prayer hall.

On the wall, a few lines in Italian, 19th century in flavour and similar in mood to the verse in the Scola Levantina, exhort the faithful to prayer: "*Humble in action and with firm faith / Come every pious man to speak your prayers / And though you later turn your steps elsewhere / Always keep your thoughts turned to God*". The prayer hall itself is preceded by a kind of vestibule similar to that in the Scola Canton; since the synagogue was founded it has served as a passage, a waiting room and a meeting place, but it may over the years have housed certain particular ceremonies, since it is in touch with the prayer hall through large sliding windows in the dividing wall. Near the entrance is a washbasin and a collection box; round the walls run some benches, and on the wall overlooking Rio di Ghetto Nuovo is an inscription recording the synagogue's 1739-40 renovation: "*In the time of the illustrious Rabbi Isacco Pacifico, preacher and example of justice / the synagogue was renovated / in the year 5499 (1739) / and the respectable par-*

nasim of the community / with great honour and great feasting / returned to the synagogue on the Sabbath before / the first day of the month of Nisan / 5500 (1740); / these are their names / Samuele, son of Aronne Ha-Kohen / Isaia, son of the illustrious Rabbi Salomone Nizza / Elia, son of the rabbi Benedetto Osimo".

Venice - Ghetto Nuovo: Scola Italiana, façade on the Campo

The Italian Jews' prayer hall does not display any particularly original overall design comparable to the rich refinement of the Scola Grande Tedesca, the discreet harmony of the Scola Canton or the imposing magnificence of the Scola Levantina. Nevertheless, it finds its unifying element in the broad luminosity provided by the five large windows opening onto the Campo di Ghetto Nuovo, which manage to blend harmoniously with the sense of calm austerity conferred on the surroundings by the neutral colouring of the decorative details, carefully maintained by successive renovations over the years. The luminous effect — perhaps not divorced in conception from the mystical atmosphere created in the Ghetto by the activity, between 1574 and 1580, of Menaḥem A. da Fano — can be absorbed as a whole, due both to the interior spatial design — which, though bifocal, with 'aron and bimah facing each other, is nevertheless almost square, without the arrangement of the pews for worshippers forming a sort of dividing aisle in the middle as they do in other synagogues — and also to the position of the entrance, in the centre of the south wall, which allows the entire architectural complex, within the controlled proportions of the structures, to be taken in at a glance. The atmosphere of balanced sobriety is ensured by the careful colour scheme used in the wooden panelling on the lower part of the walls — with benches and decorative panels of shaped octagons punctuated by light Corinthian columns — attributable, very probably, to the 1739-40 restoration, and by the ornamental squares, on a lighter background, on the upper section of the walls, each one of which has in the centre, on darker stone, an inscription of which the acrostic indicates the name of a certain 'Abhraham, for whom *shalom* (peace) is requested at the beginning of every last line. The whole epigraphic display on the upper section of the hall is the gift, probably in 1810, of Yitzḥaq Norzi (-a) to honour the memory of his father; this can be worked out (Cassuto) from the acrostic of the inscription above the entrance, which records the contribution of certain worshippers in work and money "to match the splendour of the house of God with the splendour of its decoration". A number of light pilasters like slender Corinthian columns, Renaissance in style, arranged in parallel rows on the north and south sides, link the wooden panels with a cornice that runs right round the hall, broken by an arch over each of the two focal points, and with a fine ceiling, perhaps attributable to the 18th century restoration, decorated with areas of solid colour, in perfect harmony with the rest of the decor. The women's gallery fits well into this complex, after a design similar to that used in the Scola Canton and the Scola Levantina. It was moved from its original location and placed beside the *bimah*, above the entrance vestibule (after 1609) and punctuated with lowered gratings in symmetry with the large square windows in the dividing wall, which let light into the calm, severe prayer hall. (Some documents show that until 1929 its interior was adorned with Hebrew inscriptions on leather, bearing in acrostic the name of 'Abhraham and the word *shalom* at the beginning of the last line. But the connection with the wall inscriptions in the prayer hall, and the origin and source of these leather strips, given the particular content of the lines, remains, for the present, in doubt [see page 95]).

61

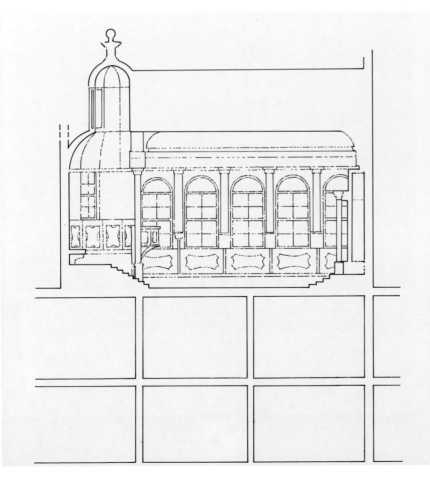

Venice - Ghetto Nuovo: Scola Italiana (section)

Once again, however, the two focal points of *'aron* and *bimah*, facing each other, remain the hall's major points of attraction, the less showy in this case being the *'aron*. The present fixture is surrounded and cut off from the rest of the hall by a wooden balustrade with stylized columns, closed by a little gate ornamented with fine, intercrossing arches, "*gift and work*" as the inscription says, "*of Menaḥem J. Guglielmi*" in the year 5602 (1842). Since the 18th century, but with extensive alterations dating mainly from the early 19th century, it has replaced an earlier, smaller Ark of the Covenant, the doors of which, finely decorated inside and out, were rediscovered hidden in a safe place in the synagogue and recently reused in a restored structure to adorn the small community temple at Mestre. As indicated on the central section of the base, the present *'aron* was the gift of Beniamino Marina di Consiglio. Its doors have decorative appliqué panels on the outside and the Ten Commandments carved on the inside. It is framed by a composition of wooden elements in imitation of antique Renaissance schemes, preceded by four steps, and embellished with four Corinthian columns on high bases, which support an architrave of classical style with touches of baroque, framing the typical ornament of a crown.

The ensemble fits perfectly between the decorative wall sections, beneath the arch which serves to accentuate it and forms part of the cornice that adorns the entire hall (but now hidden behind a heavy canopy). It conceals a tiny room, today separated from the prayer hall, which in the early layout of the synagogue may perhaps have served the purpose of housing the Scrolls of the Law.

62

Venice - Ghetto Nuovo: Scola Italiana, the *'aron*

Venice - Ghetto Nuovo: Scola Italiana, the *bimah* ▶

Opposite the *'aron* and considerably more impressive, stands the *bimah*, which no doubt recalls designs in the nearby Scola Canton. The combined result of successive alterations to the temple, the structure occupies about six metres of wall space, standing out from it to a depth of three metres, on a platform nearly a metre and a half above the level of the hall floor, and almost constituting a separate environment from the area in front of it. Accentuated, like the *'aron*, by an arch that interrupts the hall's decorative cornice, framed by four high-based Corinthian columns, and raised by eight finely ornate steps, a small *bimah* stands in front of a wide, polygonal apse whose walls are divided horizontally into three bands of colour in perfect harmony with the hall's overall colour scheme. The lower band continues the wooden wall panelling with benches and decorated panels, providing distinctive seating for the *parnasim* and the notables. The central seat stands out, crowned with a simple arch. The middle band in imitation marble echoes the other frames with inscriptions, featuring tablets similarly coloured but here with words referring to the specific duties of the officiants and their public behaviour. The top section includes a small lantern opening beneath the umbrella-shaped cupola, allowing light to filter down on the spot from which the *Torah* is read out. The entire concept can in all probability be attributed to the 18th century restoration, but a shell-shaped inscription on the lower part of the *bimah* says "*the dais in the house of our Lord was renovated in the year 5569 (1809)*" the period from which dates the whole middle band and, perhaps, the finishing of the columns. A salient and distinctive trait is the frequency with which writing is used as decoration; although not an integral part of the architecture, it constitutes in every case a sign of a quest for originality, even in modest art work, on the part of the Italian Jews.

63

The settlement of the "Ponentine nation" (from the West, hence Spanish) in the Ghetto Vecchio was the second great event of the late 16th century, destined to radically change the face of the Venetian Jewish quarter. They were perhaps the richest people of the *Università* and a good number of them were converts to Christianity, baptized Jews, known as *marrani* ("converts" or "new Christians"), who later, publicly or secretly, returned to the practice of Judaism. There is some controversy about their arrival in Venice and their settlement in the Ghetto, since surviving documents afford only a very general idea of events.

Their vicissitudes go back at least to the late 14th century. It is known, in fact, that at that date Iberian Jews, after centuries of serene and prosperous existence marked by the highest products of medieval Hebrew culture, were subjected to violent persecution, mainly on the part of the Dominicans, which took the form of compulsory sermons, the prohibition of Talmudic studies, or enforced conversions. Many converts remained privately faithful to the practice of Judaism but if they were discovered and hauled before the Inquisition they had to suffer public execution by burning at the stake (known as an *auto da fé* — act of faith). After a century of torment, when King Ferdinand seized power, they were given a drastic choice: either leave their lands and make for safer shores on the Mediterranean, or really abandon their religion and embrace the Catholic faith. Many at once chose the path of exile, amongst them the noble Abrabanel family who went to Venice. Many, on the other hand, became "new Christians" secure in the consolidation of their wealth by exploiting the new circumstances in their commercial activity, since they were able to take advantage both of the close network established between the Mediterranean towns where their old brethren had settled, and of the wide markets opened to them by their joining the new confession. But even this was a brief illusion. The Spanish Inquisition became harsher, and in the end they too left not only the Iberian peninsula but also

64

their new religion, returning to the practice of Judaism, albeit often only in private (crypto-Jews), and scattering to more appealing ports.

Obviously Venice was once again one of the poles of major attraction, this time for the Sephardim; their relations with the Ghetto environment and, even more, with the Rialto commercial centre, were among the strongest the new arrivals succeeded in establishing. The Republic had to face a decidedly new situation, and its first reaction was negative; religious suspicion on the one hand and economic rivalry and jealousy on the other persuaded *La Serenissima* to drive out the new Christians in 1497, but by then it was inevitable that the dense network of ties already created would, in the event, favour the settled presence in the city of *marrani* — often already "going Jewish" again — with the tacit toleration of the government. For half a century the unstable situation persisted without modification or interference until, in 1550, under heavy pressure from the Church and the influence exercised by Emperor Charles V, Venice was constrained to decree a further expulsion of the group, who had by then become numerous and influential.

But it at once became obvious that the Venetian economy would have to pay too high a price for their expulsion, and the Rialto companies, squeezed between Venetian merchants and new Christians, intervened to ask for the measure to be revoked. *La Serenissima* backed up certain Inquisition censors in order to combat "new Christianity" in the face of informers' accusations, often hard to verify, but went back on its decision, conceding, with evident opportunism, the maintenance of present commercial relations with the Ponentines, on condition they did not come to live and "nest" in the Veneto domain. It was yet another compromise solution, consistent with the Senate's traditional pragmatism, but it was tantamount to admitting the economic importance of the new Jewish group, its wealth and the weight it carried in Venetian society, all factors which would sooner or later lead to official recognition of their presence in the city. This indeed came about in 1573 — in sharp contrast to what was happening in the rest of the country — when many "new Christians" had already strategically infiltrated the Levantine group. It seems that the Venetian Holy Office, whose trials often involved Jews or crypto-Jews, presented no real obstacle to the decision; its very composition, a mixture of ecclesiastical and lay members, was particularly susceptible to non-religious, social and economic reasoning, and the deeds of the Inquisition itself, almost a mirror of the compromise between Church and State in Venice — a State not fettered by formal political influence from the Church, but still always a Catholic State (Pullan) — may in fact explain the not wholly intransigent attitude adopted in its verdicts and the mildness of the sentences it pronounced (Ioly Zorattini). So, after a flood of immigration to the Venetian islands of yet more *marrani* in 1580, this time from Ferrara, and under acute pressure from Daniel Rodriga, appointed Consul of the Hebrew "nation" by Doge Alvise Mocenigo in January 1574, also in consideration of the strong advantages brought to Venice by the Levantines' work in association with the Sephardic group, the *condotta* granted in 1589 came as a readily predictable denouement to the drama. It also recognized the Ponentines as an independent "nation" admitted to the Ghetto Vecchio. The troubled history of the Spanish Jews on the Lagoon was to conclude with their acquisition of a settled status that would shortly make the Sephardim the dominant group in the Venetian Ghetto.

◀ 15th C. Portuguese *'aron*, now in Leghorn (Via Micali)

New York - Pierpont Morgan Library: The caravels that carried the Jews expelled from Spain (Neapolitan Codex, 15th C.)

65

The first *condotta* granted to the Levantines and Ponentines is a milestone in the evolution of the Venetian Ghetto. The strong Sephardic contingent were very different in culture, custom and tradition, also in wealth and commercial activity, from their Ashkenazi cousins, and in a distinctly privileged economic position compared with the other nation; their official admission was to modify the overall structure of the segregated quarter, turning the Ghetto Nuovo and the Ghetto Vecchio into two separate units controlled, furthermore, by two different authorities, the former by the *Cattaver* and the latter by the *Cinque Savi alla Mercanzia*, who were often in pursuit of different aims.

Actually, the *condotta* in its brief articles outlined remarkably advantageous conditions such as the German group would never totally succeed in obtaining.

Having conceded safe conduct and freedom of worship protected from harassment, the text went on to assure the merchants of every possibility of movement, emigratory or immigratory, insofar as the lands under Venetian dominion were concerned; notice of a year and a half should the State make decisions of expulsion, so that all outstanding economic matters could be wound up; protection equal to that of any other Venetian citizen in case of war; and the guarantee of non-interference in the "nation's" internal administration whatever direction it wished to take. Of course they were privileges that the Senate, obviously spurred by economic motives, would not have been prepared to grant except on terms of clear guarantees; and the document concluded by stating, with preventive intent, that in order to be considered as a member of the Levantine or Ponentine "nations" it was necessary to have first been received, with full responsibility, by the "nation" itself, and to have obtained the approval of at least four of the *Cinque Savi alla Mercanzia*. But even within these limitations, comparison with the well circumscribed space within which the Ashkenazi nation had been obliged to move from its very first *condotta* reveals remarkable differences. Friction between the two "nations" although hidden and restrained, was inevitable, and their everyday rivalries were a distinctive part of the Ghetto's internal "little history".

The 1589 *condotta* was not only a political act issued by a State motivated by obvious opportunism, but also a document actively sought and almost suggested as implicit recognition of credit acquired by the most able and influential of the Sephardim in the Ghetto, namely Daniel Rodriga, whom Doge Alvise Mocenigo had appointed Consul and representative of the Hebrew nation in January 1574, for having "rendered excellent service". With, above all, the opening of the port of Spalato (today's Split), suggested and partly subsidized by him to eliminate competition from Ancona and Ragusa (today's Dubrovnik) and reduce the danger of pirate attack, and the resumption of relations with the West and the constant demonstration, therefore, of the need for Jewish commercial contributions, he had in fact prepared the ground to secure for his co-religionists the best possible conditions and the widest guarantees of stability. Echoing, therefore, a petition from the merchants themselves and a personal appeal of his own, he could venture so far as to suggest to the State, in a precise proposal, the terms of the future *condotta*, which would later be largely endorsed by the *Cinque Savi*. In five clearly worded paragraphs Rodriga requested absolute freedom of movement throughout the Veneto domain, the free exercise of the Jewish religion, even for those who had elsewhere professed another (meaning the *marrani*), due notice in case of decrees of banishment, protection in case of war, permission to have their own internal administration, and exemption from all contributions to the running of the pawnbrokers' shops in order to mark the difference from the German "nation". In return he promised extreme severity, under the control of the "authority" in accepting those who applied for admittance to the Levantine or Ponentine "nations". Comparison between the text of the Consul's proposals and that of the *condotta* reveals surprising conformity. How much the Sephardim owe to this "president" of their community is beyond dispute.

Condotta a favor Noſtro.

1589. 17. Luglio. In Pregadi.

L'Anderà Parte, che per Anni dieci proſſimi venturi ſia conceſſo ſalvo Condotto a qualunque Ebreo Mercante Levantino, e Ponentino di poter venire ad abitar in queſta Città noſtra, con le loro Famiglie, ſtar, & in eſſa praticare liberamente la Seſſa overo la Baretta Zala da Ebrei, nel qual poſſano uſare, e far li loro Ritti, Precetti, Cerimonie, e tenire Sinagoghe ſecondo l' uſo loro, ſicuri per detto tempo di non eſſer moleſtati per Cauſa de Religione da qual ſi voglia Magiſtrato.

Ommiſſis.

Et acciochè tra eſſa Nazione non ſiano admeſſi ſe

קצין וראש לכל עמו
לו הוא דורש טוב מעצמו
כי דמשרה עלי שכמו
שמו הגביר כמ"ר דניאל רודרינה נסטר ביום כ"ז
סיון השס"ג תנצב ה:

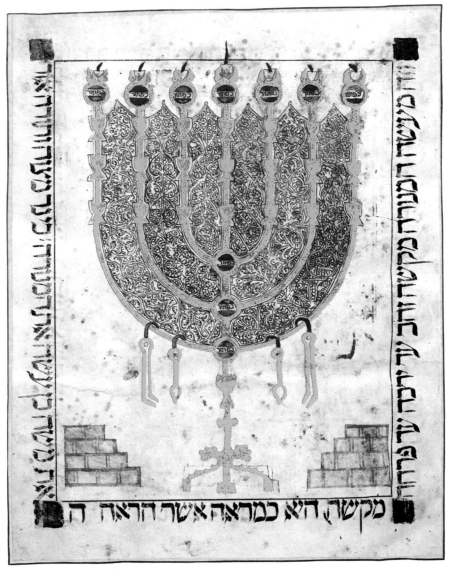

London - British Library: *Menorah* (7-branched lamp) from a Spanish Bible of 1384

Venice - Safeconduct granted to the Levantines and Ponentines (Sephardim) on 27 July 1589 (detail of an 18th C. print). (Original in Venetian State Archives, *Senato Mar*, filza 104, 27 July 1589)

Venice, Lido - Old Jewish Cemetery: Text of the gravestone of Daniel Rodriga, d.27 siwan (May-June) 5363 (1603)

The new Ponentine "nation" received in the Ghetto tacitly at first, then officially, succeeded at once, through their own cultural and economic merit, in winning a place of such pre-eminence and prestige that they began to wish to see their superiority reflected in the largest, if not the most imposing, synagogue in the Jewish quarter. Subsequently, theirs was to remain the one and only synagogue serving the whole quarter.

When and how they founded it is hard to say because of the paucity of surviving documentation and the lack of inscriptions in any way connected with building or restoration — as exist in the nearby Scola Levantina. All the same it is reasonable to suppose that, throughout the 16th century, given their particular situation, the *marrani* the large group of converts present in Venice, never once publicly exposed themselves in a dedicated and easily identifiable building to celebrate their traditional rituals and ceremonies. Almost certainly they would have preferred instead to use small private prayer rooms, easily camouflaged for obvious motives of caution, until, in the 1580s, their status became so stable that they could afford to build a public synagogue capable of holding a fairly large number of worshippers.

The present temple can be attributed, on stylistic grounds, to the mid 17th century, but it can be argued that they did not wait until that date to construct the public prayer hall and were not without a single centre of co-ordination for more than half a century. On the basis of such conjectures it seems reasonable to suggest that the most probable dating for the building's foundation is actually 1584, that is to say just a few years before the *condotta* that made the Ponentine presence in the Ghetto official. This is in fact the earliest date mentioned in the documents available, recorded in this particular connection as that when the "*Congregation of the Ponentines*" was begun, that is, the Scola's *Talmudh Torah*, as it was then called. In an inventory, *Archivio della Scuola K.K.T.T. dei Ponentini* (*Archives of the K.K.T.T. School of the Ponen-*

67

tines), written up in 1778 by the scribe Simon Bueno, catalogued under the letter L is "Libro primo" (Book One) of the "parts" of the Ponentine *Università* from that very year 5344 (1584) until 5361 (1601), therefore affording fairly convincing evidence. This dating is indicated only by Roth and without any documentary support, but seems more likely than other scholars' proposals such as Ottolenghi's (1533) and Pinkerfeld's (1555), which have not found substantiation in any archives or writings, at least not by the present stage of research.

From that very date, then, it can be supposed that the Ponentine *Talmudh Torah* acquired the configuration and hierarchic structure not documented by any specific text, but suggested by the data obtainable from the headings in this inventory. As far as the general structure can be perceived, it was more similar to the organizations existing in the Ghetto Nuovo, with *parnasim*, stewards and secretaries called to govern the synagogue, than to that governing the nearby Scola Levantina, but with more emphasis on the pedagogic aspect of community life. In the document in question, as in the later land registers, there are abundant references to rabbis and their salaries, and to the *midhrashim* and the places where the children (*mezà puti*) would gather for study. This was perhaps a sign that fathers who had abandoned and then returned to their former faith devoted themselves more zealously than in other "nations" to imparting an integrated and more orthodox education to the next generation, in order to avoid heretical deviations or dispersions such as were, in fact, not unknown in other "new Christian" settlements. It was also a sign of a continuing sincere desire for an effective link with the most authentic religious and liturgical tradition, probably never totally forgotten.

The present synagogue was constructed, like that of the Ghetto Nuovo, on the top floor of an already existing building, which held many other halls and small rooms, giving it a multifunctional character not possessed by the nearby Levantine site. It has no connection with the early prayer hall erected by the Ponentines in the late 16th century. It certainly reveals the sense of emphatic twin focus that an extensive number of scholars tend to define as a typically western European design, if not distinctly Spanish, but it equally exhibits such typically theatrical effects in such affinity with schemes in nearby Venetian palaces, as to suggest once again the direct adoption of local motifs characterized by a firmly baroque style, rather than the revival of an independent tradition still living in the memory after the traumatic events of over a

century of migrations. Nor have precisely documented 19th century alterations, though oriented towards quite a different conception of the interior space, radically affected the basic structure of a design that every chronological fact and stylistic detail leads one to suppose is attributable to the hand of Longhena or some other artist close to his "manner" (Gaspari?). Perhaps the only link with the 16th century prayer hall is the longitudinal, bifocal plan, which to some extent limited the architect's opportunities for invention, together with the usual reasons of orientation.

It is hard to say how the early design of the Scola Spagnola looked. Only the already quoted land register of 1713 perhaps prompts a guess at a likely appearance in its description of the houses in the Campiello delle Scuole

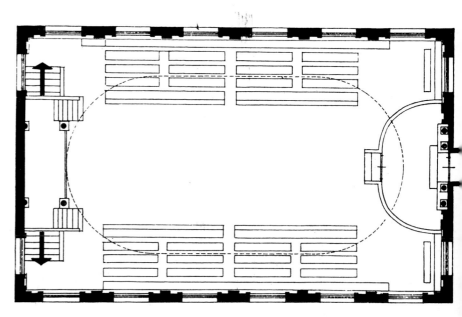

Venice - Ghetto Vecchio: Scola Spagnola, floorplan (app. 13m x 21m)

68

and the Strada Maestra. Beneath the present prayer hall it indicates the existence of a few large rooms with adjoining passages already used at that time as schools for young boys. They were spacious and windowed, and it might be suggested that the largest of them, on the first floor of the present building, was actually the Ponentines' early prayer hall. It was transversely symmetrical and bifocal, with the *'aron* and the *bimah* situated on the long sides, and must have been already fairly large if we are to believe the testimony of Leon Modena in his *Autobiografia*, when the rabbi refers to a sermon of his in the presence of many foreigners, including the French King's brother, in the "Talmudh Torah of the Sephardim" in 1629. But these guesses are hard to verify.

Possible to fix with greater certainty, however, is the construction date of the

present day baroque synagogue. Once again the jumble of scholars' conjectures is fairly extensive. Roth has 1635, Pinkerfeld 1654 and Morpurgo 1655, the latter two suggested by *Il Corriere Israelitico* of 1894 and picked up, with slight variations, by nearly all successive historians (Sandri-Alazraki, Cassuto, etc). All the suggestions are possible on the basis of texts available today and careful comparisons of style, through which it is at least possible to fix earliest and latest limits beyond which it is not reasonable to go. In the afore-mentioned 1713 land register, after a description of the Scola that corresponds exactly to what we can see today, there is added: "And Isach Pessa, Rabbi, swore in Hebrew fashion that the said Scola and buildings were made and established before the year 1661 in the same form in which they are now found, apart from the casket of Bibles and certain embellishments". And if this documentary information is allied with stylistic considerations, albeit less reliable, which lead, for example, to arguments about how the continuous white line module which connotes the exterior decoration makes its appearance among the ornamental Venetian baroque features in about the 1630s, then it is easy to deduce that the most convincing chronological placing falls very elastically within the second thirty years of the 17th century, in the period that, in this case, coincides with that of Longhena's mature work, thereby neatly justifying the attribution of the "Scola" to the author of the Madonna della Salute and the Ca' Pesaro, always mentioned in a long oral tradition but never documented.

Of late baroque origin, therefore, the synagogue only underwent marginal or partial retouching during the 18th century, such as the *'aron* doors that bear the date 1755, which did not affect the overall appearance. The only important alteration was the opening, in 1733, on the left-hand side of the wide ground-floor entrance hall, of a *midhrash* which, in the 19th century, was to be adorned with the entire decorative furnishings from the demolished Scola Kohanim in the Ghetto Nuovo.

Only in the 19th century, at a time of emancipation but also in a phase of wide assimilation, were there any important alterations that temporarily changed the original concept. In 1838, definitely through the influence of non-Jewish ideas, the knight Treves de Bonfil, against strong opposition, decided to introduce a female choir into the synagogue. Nearly sixty years later (1893-94) the architects Pellegrino Oreffice and Consiglio Fano brought about interior modifications which, although consolidating and embellishing the centuries-old decorations (ceiling, columns, walls, hangings, etc.), by the addition around the *'aron* of an area within a wooden balustrade, raised two steps above floor level, in order to place the officiant's lectern there, and the entirely unreasonable installation of the organ and choir in the place of the 69 *bimah*, with consequent transformations inside and out, altered the more genuine Sephardic feeling of space, all depending on twin focus, and substituted completely atypical hybrid ideas remote from any Jewish tradition.

Returning to the original was therefore the prime incentive guiding the more aware rabbis and *parnasim* in the 1970s, though against barely comprehensible resistance and reluctance. In 1980, the abolition of the choir brought about the renovation of the ancient *bimah*, while the restoration of the entire complex, started in 1983, has permitted the full maintenance of the 17th century structure without other deviations or arbitrary changes.

Unlike the nearby monumental Scola Levantina, the Spanish synagogue is inconspicuous from outside, jostled by the surrounding buildings and connected, inside, to the building below. The motifs of the wide, arched windows are symmetrically crowned with small, shelving architraves — echoing the decorative scheme of the continuous white cornice — and with smaller, square windows above, which skilfully break up the light moving over the walls; although each is emphasized by the typical baroque feature of a white frame, they do not seem to impinge scenographically on the visual impression of the campiello nor on the Strada Maestra in the way the Levantine façade does.

70 The façade is divided neatly into two sections by the continuous white line connecting the bottom of the windows, virtually signalling the addition of the synagogue hall on top of the former inhabited floors. The lower part is marked only by the windows of the old schoolrooms and, to one side — obviously because of the position of the building itself and the already existing structures — by a fine doorway, beautifully decorated with geometrical designs in high relief, very similar in composition to the portal of the Scola Levantina. On the arch is another verse from the *Psalms:* " *'Ashrey yoshebhey beythekha 'odh yehalelukha selah — Blessed are they who dwell in Thy house: they will be still praising Thee. Selah"* (*Psalm* LXXXIV, 5). Now, underlining the distinction between the two floors, a tablet has been set up, in a prominent position, to the everlasting memory of those deported to the Nazi death camps during the Second World War.

The entrance leads to a wide rectangular vestibule with a fine, wooden beamed ceiling and long wooden benches at the sides, which suggest that it was once used as a meeting room if not as a study room. There is a washbasin to the right, and many tablets round the walls commemorating eminent spokesmen of the Sephardic community, alongside one recording the 1893 restoration of the synagogue, and yet another, on the short side by the main door, in memory of Venetian deportees of 1943-44, near which, on the right, is the entrance to a small *sukkah* and the stairs up to the present women's gallery.

Venice - Ghetto Vecchio: Scola Spagnola, Façade on the Campiello delle Scuole

Venice - Ghetto Vecchio: Scola Spagnola, Entrance stair

horn were attracted back to Venice by the conditions offered there (Poliakov), thus swelling the number of students in the Ponentine schools. This event happened in 1732, and two dates carved among the decorations on the doorposts, 5496 (1736) to the right, and 5493 (1733) to the left, would seem to be linked to it. Over the arch is a verse from *Psalms*: "*Zeh hashsha'ar la 'A. tzaddiqim yabho'u bho — This is the gate of the Lord: the righteous shall enter into it*" (*Psalm* CXVIII, 20), as at the Scola Levantina, and on the architrave, once more like the Scola of the "wayfarers": "*Pithḥu-li sha'arey - tzedheq — Open to me the gates of righteousness*" (*Psalm* CXVIII, 19) and "*'Anna' 'A. hoshi 'ah nna' — Save now, we beseech Thee, O Lord*" (*Psalm* CXVIII, 25). All these clearly allusive verses are from the *Hallel*, the sequence of *Psalms* CXIII - CXVIII which are sung — not necessarily in their entirety — during the three "feasts of pilgrimage" (Passover, Pentecost and the Feast of the Tabernacles), *Ḥanukkah* and the first of every month. This is the small room that, during the great restoration of the synagogue in 1893, was furnished with the fittings from the demolished *Scola Kohanim* in the Ghetto Nuovo.

Facing it is the staircase leading to the floor above, its bronze gates lending it a solemn appearance. The spacious, theatre-like effect, assisted by the controlled colour scheme, is emphasized by two calmly imposing curtained doorways after the first landing, opening directly into the prayer hall. The ancient alms box is still on the wall near the doors which afford access to the rooms where, according to the evidence of 1713, the wardens used to hold meetings or men gathered for study. The entire complex, although accepted as typically religious, inevitably makes one think of the influence of the lay designs of the grand Venetian palaces (Cassuto), with the entrance on the ground floor and the staircase leading to the main floor (as in the Scola Levantina). This is perhaps further confirmation of Sephardic open-mindedness towards local culture, already far removed from respect for their own tradition.

71

The two longer sides appear more important. A wide doorway on the left opens into a small study of elongated rectangular shape, probably arranged as a *midhrash* in the early 18th century, when a group of Sephardim from Leg-

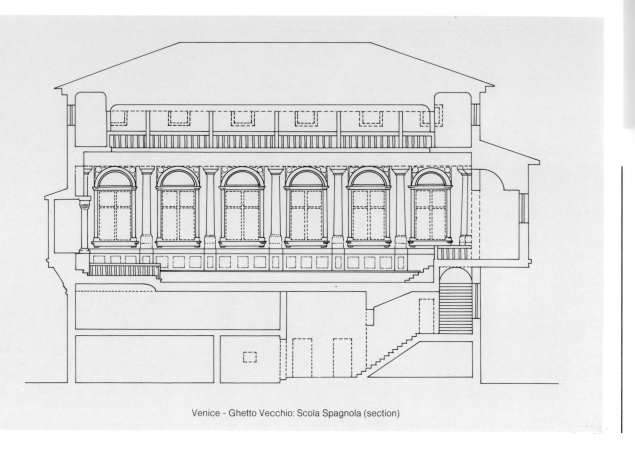

Venice - Ghetto Vecchio: Scola Spagnola (section)

The Ponentine is the largest and most flamboyant of all the Ghetto synagogues, but it and the Scola Canton also come closest to an "internal" concept, more typically Jewish, revolving around an idea of integration between man and space.

It is constructed on a strictly bifocal plan, with the 'aron and the bimah facing each other on the short sides of an almost perfect rectangle, and seems to be connected, albeit indirectly, with the ancient, local model of the desert Tabernacle, the arcane seat of the divinity, but interprets its empty space in a "historicized" key, making it "live" through man, who prays and studies in it, and takes the beat of his liturgical "tempo" from it day by day. The instruments of such an interpretation are those offered to the imaginative observer by the "illusory" sense of the space itself, suggested by the baroque style of the decorative and ornamental features that succeed in conferring an intimate unity on the surroundings.

The two focal points are conceptually joined together by the wooden pews round the walls and wooden panelling up to the height of the windows. The benches for worshippers are arranged parallel to the long sides, leaving a wide open space in the middle, characteristic of nearly all the Venetian synagogues, where a carpet runner can be laid with the object of linking the two poles. The floor is soberly decorated with white and grey tiles geometrically arranged in a repetitive pattern of concentric squares, creating a sensation of intimate cohesion between the surrounding walls. The finely ornate ceiling does almost the same, attempting to suggest a similar sense of unity with high reliefs in wood and stucco and a huge chandelier in the centre, reminiscent, from a distance, of the sumptuous decorations in Ca' Pesaro.

But what mostly creates the cohesion between the parts is the unifying function of the women's gallery — reached by an internal staircase that was substituted for the outside one in the last century — similar to that in the Scola Grande Tedesca but probably boasting the prestige of antedating the Ashkenazi one. It is elliptical, decorated with a balustrade with wooden banisters and a loggia with a cornice and gilded crowns — a shining example of Venetian baroque — and surrounds the prayer hall to its full width, managing to create not only a perfect degree of integration between the section reserved for women and the place of prayer, but also a masterly scenographic effect, not perhaps unmindful of similar designs in Venetian theatres, and fully in tune with 17th century taste.

The vast complex thus created is integrated and given a note of unifying colour by the large, arched windows with their red curtains hanging uninterruptedly down the walls and, between them, the skilful interplay of panels, columns and marble pilaster strips vertically linking the wooden parts of the hall.

The entire decorative scheme compensates magnificently for the total absence of inscriptions or epigraphs, but never appears excessive or grandiose, on account of its unusual airiness and composure. It is undoubtedly the work of an expert and gifted mind, surely close to Longhena. The taste, the stylistic scheme, the overall effect that makes an immediate impact on the worshipper — because the off-centre entrance, on two sides of the bimah, leads into direct contact with the hall — all confirm this without any possible doubt.

In short, the Ponentines, like the Levantines, decided to display their wealth and cultural weight by erecting — whether or not they resorted to the principal school builder — the school of major prestige in the Venice of their time.

The hall's two focal points are perfectly integrated into the ensemble, one might almost say "on a human scale" (Cassuto), and not imposing or overbearing as elsewhere.

The 'aron, once more cleverly relying on the skilful use of coloured marbles, is a structure composed of classical elements remodelled in baroque form. It is framed, almost engulfed in what looks like a brilliant starry sky under a wide triumphal arch, and supported by pilasters on which is written in golden letters: "Da' liphney mi 'atah 'omedh — Think before Whom thou standest" (Talmudh, Berakhoth, 28b). The composition is horizontally divided into three: resting on high pedestals, four columns of striated black marble with Corinthian capitals and surmounted by a tympanum enclose the actual Ark of the Covenant, the doors of which bear, besides the Ten Commandments, a verse from Psalms: "Shiwwithi 'A. leneghdi thamidh — I have set the Lord always before me" (Psalm XVI, 8), and the date 1755. Above this again, emphasized by

a semi-circular frame, stand the Tablets of the Law.

The ensemble, whose features remind some people of the altar of the Cappella Vendramin at Castello, is flanked by two huge windows which complete the internal tripartite effect. It would achieve the real effect for which it was conceived had there not been added, in 1893, in place of an imposing canopy — which, according to old lithographs, covered the entire structure and the surrounding area — a semi-circular balustrade and a wooden rostrum of two steps, to house the officiant's lectern, he being obliged to leave the bimah, which had been transformed into a choir, and say the prayers in an unnatural manner, near the 'aron with his back to the congregation. The only results obtained by this have been the infringement of the authentic rapport between 'aron and hall, with an obviously divisory effect and the total disintegration of the original spatial concept. For another thing, a small tablet near the right-hand side of the

steps in front of the 'aron has had to be raised, or else it would have been hidden; it records a curious event: In 5609 (1848-49), during the Austrian seige of Venice, a bomb launched from Forte Marghera hit the synagogue during evening prayers on the 29th of 'abh (17 August), but without doing any damage. The rabbi of the time, Lattes, decided to immortalize the miraculous escape and wrote the text of the epigraph, which says: "Here penetrated a bomb, falling it embedded itself, it did no damage, it passed with violence, but with judgement. The eve of the first of 'elul, during the hour of prayer 5609". From that day on, every year on the last Friday of the month of 'abh, it has been customary to recall with special prayers the day that has passed into history as "Bomb Friday".

Venice - Ghetto Vecchio: Scola Spagnola, the 'aron

The *bimah* is far more showy, and closely linked to examples in other Venetian synagogues, but with striking concessions to theatrical effect. The pulpit, crowned by two columns with Corinthian capitals, on high plinths, is another reminder of the columns in the Jerusalem Temple, but also, some say, as in the Scola Levantina, of the celebrated altar in St Peter's, Rome. It is flanked by two short flights of wooden steps leading up to it, and backed by a vast blue dome resting on a polygonal apse, which protrudes from the body of the building at the back. Its effect, combined with the colour interplay of draperies and marbles, is certainly highly picturesque, even though less majestic than the imposing *bimah* in the Scola Levantina.

74 Unfortunately, from 1893 to 1980 — nearly a century — the scheme of decoration, in perfect conformity with the solemn sobriety of the hall, was disrupted by the addition of a choir section and the installation of an organ with pipes to accompany the liturgy. This involved extensions to the outside walls and the introduction of an overwhelming, albeit carefully geometrical, wooden fixture inside. Since 1980, in the climate of reintegration that has governed the complete restoration of the whole synagogue, the 19th century superstructure has been removed, partly anyway, in order to restore the complete structure of the entrance wall to its original appearance and the officiant's dais to its original function. Arguments unhappily divided worshippers during the restoration work but, after all, this was the only way for the synagogue to regain the distinctive twin focus of its original conception.

Venice - Ghetto Vecchio: Scola Spagnola, the *bimah* transformed into a choir 1893-1980

Venice - Ghetto Vecchio : Scola Spagnola, the *bimah* :

The setting up of two new centres for prayer and study with adjoining accommodation for primary and higher education doubtless gave incentive, even in such a hard period, to a cultural reawakening and, most importantly, to the training of a new generation of rabbis and the perpetuation of Talmudic tradition. The phenomenon of the Ashkenazi *yeshibhoth* which had characterized the first half of the 16th century, offering a veritable fortress to rabbinical orthodoxy, had gone into crisis halfway through the century at the same time, moreover, as the enforced decline and standstill of Hebrew publishing activity. Then in the last decade, under the stimulus of the newly arrived Sephardim, as soon as the situation in the Ghetto seemed to be moving towards stability, there was an effort to revive interest in religious studies with the courageous opening of two new rabbinical academies run by two scholars and preachers of vast experience and proven ability. One was entrusted to Yehudhah da Fano of Venetian and Paduan fame, and remained open from 1596 to 1606. The other, better known, was run by that rising star of 17th century Venice, Leon Modena, then little more than twenty years old; his teaching was to have a considerable influence over the whole Ghetto and among non-Jewish intellectuals.

"The Lord made me find favour with all my hearers" asserts Modena in his *Autobiografia*, "so that in the month of 'iyar 5354 (1594), when the notable gentleman Kalonimos Belgrado, of blessed memory, set up a Talmudic school and a seat of learning in the garden, I became its principal teacher, and continued so for twenty five years ... thanks be to God, winning a good reputation in all corners of the land". Thus he describes one of the earliest of his demanding public activities in the Venetian community, not to mention the opening of a phase that would within a short time have helped Venice, through the prestige of her rabbis, to win a role of primary importance in European Jewish culture. A modest wooden doorway flanked by two small windows is still to be seen in the Ghetto Vecchio on the side of the Strada Maestra where the wayfarers' houses stood, and this building is generally thought to have housed the little academy; besides holding a "biographical" curiosity as part of the famous rabbi's busy earthly affairs, it stands as a tangible sign of a will to survive that discrimination and segregation were powerless to quell.

Venice - Ghetto Vecchio: the so-called Leon Modena *Midhrash*

A page of the *haggadhah* with woodcut illustrations, published in Venice by Di Gara in 1599

Another tangible result of the cultural commitment brought about by the stabilization of the internal situation, was the courageous revival, in spite of serious obstacles, of Hebrew publishing. Launched by Bragadin and, on a smaller scale, by the Zanetti, Cavalli and Grifio families, it found in Giovanni Di Gara, as we have seen, the most worthy successor to Daniel Bomberg.

Between 1564 and 1609 he used Bomberg's own types and editors of high reputation such as Archivolti and Gershon, and published about a hundred works, notably some of the earliest illustrated Hebrew texts known, the dictionary by the well known doctor Dawidh de' Pomis, *Tzemaḥ Dawidh*, and above all the celebrated Venetian *haggadhah* (the text that is read during the Passover supper) first in 1599, then in 1609 with translations, and its woodcut illustrations were later to be copied in all the most famous Venetian *haggadhoth* in succeeding centuries right up to the present day. It was a work not reserved only for scholars' study, but aimed at more popular circulation, entering finally into daily liturgical routine to keep alive, or rekindle — especially among the "new" Sephardic Jews — a religious spirit that was really only dormant, never completely dead.

THE GHETTO VECCHIO

The definitive settlement of the two Sephardic "nations" in 1589 and 1598-99, and the erection of the great synagogues, together with the adaptation and enlargement of the existing dwellings, produced a substantial transformation in the Ghetto Vecchio, not only in the buildings, but also in the quality of life. In the beginning it was not on a closed plan, naturally isolated from the rest of the city like the Ghetto Nuovo, but on the contrary its houses, though few, and its orchards had good links with the surrounding inhabited areas, making it a natural thoroughfare, often busy and noisy, as the Levantines complained, with long lanes meeting in a central square, connecting the new foundry with the Cannaregio embankment, the site of heavy commercial traffic.

The first thing necessitated by the Sephardim arrivals, therefore, was the artificial isolation of the district, making it, in this way at least, similar to the adjoining quarter. The segregation was effected by continuing the process started in 1541 of raising a high wall all round a well defined perimeter, without altering existing buildings except for closing any windows of dwellings that might overlook the Jewish enclosure. The isolation achieved in this way, however, was never total; a portico beyond the Agudi bridge and another leading towards the Cannaregio embankment were controlled by watchmen, but they and a quay beside the Rio di Ghetto Nuovo permitted fairly rapid coming and going, unlike the gates of the Ghetto Nuovo. Furthermore, the Sephardim, rather than passively submitting to an externally imposed situation, turned it as far as possible to their own advantage, as the Ashkenazim had done, imposing on the district assigned to them the mark of Jewish prestige and the quality of their commercial activity, transforming what was there according to their needs, to some extent modifying the roads and urban plan with their own buildings, particularly the synagogue, and above all affixing the seal of their presence on placenames, which were linked for centuries with the most reputable Spanish and Levantine families.

As most of them had work that involved travelling, or a business in constant fluid rapport with the Venetian and Mediterranean commercial centres, thus requiring continual movement outside the Ghetto, they endowed the district with a residential character, raising the houses round the courtyards, lanes and little square sometimes as high as nine storeys — the so-called "Ghetto skyscrapers" — and opening a limited number of shops and public buildings strictly in response to local need, such as the inn, the hospital, the bookshop and various groceries and butchers, whereas the Ghetto Nuovo district, dependent on pawnbroking and the rag-and-bone trade aimed at an outside clientele, was always emphasizing its attractive commercial aspect, generally tending towards the centre, with three banks and a multitude of shops open from dawn to sunset to non-Jewish customers.

In practice, therefore, it was the very nature of the economic commitments to which the inmates were obliged or traditionally inclined that determined the different urban quality of the two areas of segregation. Although life in each was governed by similar impositions and timetables, with the opening of the gates in the morning and their closure at nightfall, with restrictions and daily checks, nevertheless the Ghetto Nuovo, out of its need to survive, changed from a naturally closed environment into an open pole of attraction, while the Ghetto Vecchio, once a virtually open space and a thoroughfare, changed into an artificially closed environment reserved for people who carried on their daily work away from it. The liturgical "tempo" of the synagogue (Bonfil), whose rhythm punctuated life on the island around San Girolamo, was overlaid, though not smothered, by an entirely bourgeois "merchants' tempo" (Le Goff) which governed life in the lanes of the Ghetto Vecchio, as if to mark a distance, in this respect also, that only time would arduously succeed in bridging.

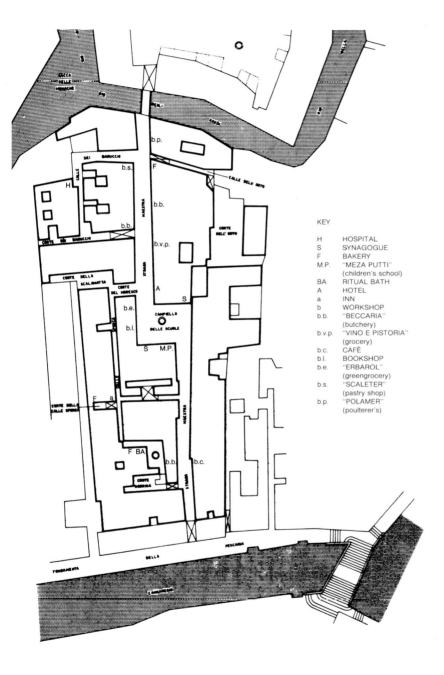

KEY

H	HOSPITAL
S	SYNAGOGUE
F	BAKERY
M.P.	"MEZA PUTTI" (children's school)
BA	RITUAL BATH
A	HOTEL
a	INN
b	WORKSHOP
b.b.	"BECCARIA" (butchery)
b.v.p.	"VINO E PISTORIA" (grocery)
b.c.	CAFÈ
b.l.	BOOKSHOP
b.e.	"ERBAROL" (greengrocery)
b.s.	"SCALETER" (pastry shop)
b.p.	"POLAMER" (poulterer's)

The Ghetto Vecchio stretches longi-
tudinally from the Rio di Ghetto Nuovo
(Rio degli Agudi) and the Cannaregio
embankment (Fondamenta della Pescaria) and consists of dissimilar
groups of houses, sometimes in a maze
of courtyards and alleys about the axis
of Calle di Ghetto Vecchio, Campiello
delle Scuole and Calle di Ghetto Vecchio again (formerly Strada Maestra,
Campiello del Pozzo, Strada Maestra).
The surrounding wall, which followed
the entire artificially delineated perimeter, excluded the last row of houses
facing the Pescaria embankment,
which belonged to Christian families
and were not only lower but also distinguished by a cross on the roof from the
neighbouring tall Jewish houses, indicated by coats of arms or plaques in
Hebrew.

Entrance was by way of the two
porticos, one near the Agudi bridge,
now demolished, the other cutting
through the row of houses overlooking
the Cannaregio embankment, still there,
with the traces of the locking gates
and the window, now bricked up, from
which the watchman used to keep his
vigil. The central axis was the site of
frequently used public buildings such
as foodshops, a bookshop in the Campiello, an inn with twenty four rooms
near the Scola Levantina, and the bakery for unleavened bread near the
bridge in the alley called the Calle del
Forno (oven lane). Round it clustered
the lanes and courtyards onto which
looked private dwellings, with no set
plan, but marking the most of the space
available.

With the Agudi bridge behind, the
Calle and the *Corte dell'Orto* (orchard
lane and court) opened out on the left,
and the *Calle* and the *Corte dei Barucchi* (the Barukh family courtyard),
where the Ghetto hospital stood, on the
right. Going along the Strada Maestra,
before reaching the *Campiello delle
Scuole* (schools' square), formerly del
Pozzo (well), there were, to the right, the
entrances to the Scola Levantina and
the *Albergo dei Viandanti* (Wayfarers'
Inn), the *Corte del Moresco* (Moor's
court), which led to the *Calle Sporca*
(dirty alley) and the courtyard of the

77

Venetian State Archives: Building with three-
mullioned window in the Ghetto Vecchio, near the
bridge Agudi (*Ufficiali al Cattaver*, b. 279)

Map of the Ghetto Vecchio from a 1711 land
register (Venetian State Archives, *Savi alle Decime*, b. 433)

78

same name, and the *Corte Scalamatta* (crazy stair yard). After crossing the Campiello and going along the rest of the Strada Maestra, just before the portico, on the right, was the entrance to the *Corte Rodriga* (Rodriguez family), almost like an indipendent "citadel" with its own public well, its ritual baths and its bakery for unleavened bread.

It was a complicated and intricate tangle, but certainly more fit to live in than the suffocating dwellings of the Ghetto Nuovo.

Venice - Ghetto Vecchio: Campiello delle Scuole

Venice - Ghetto Vecchio: Calle di Ghetto Vecchio, looking towards Cannaregio

Apart from these details, it is without doubt the placenames of the Sephardic quarter that show a decided difference from the area round San Girolamo. The most striking fact is that most of the 17th and 18th century names of its alleys and courtyards seem to be those of relatively famous Jewish families who lived in them and only rarely do we find more general, common names. Certainly the *Calle dell'Orto* and the *Calle Sporca* and the *Strada Maestra* itself reveal that their names came from their specific local character, and it has been ascertained that the *Corte Scalamatta* too owes its name to the existence, in the overlooking "skyscraper" of a typically Venetian "crazy" staircase, dark and twisting, connecting a large number of entrances in the same building, rather than commemorating, as some would have it, an undocumented *Calamatta* family.

But most placenames certainly originated from the presence of families residing in the Ghetto for a considerable time. *Calle dei Barucchi* recalls a *Barukh* family, while the family *Rodriguez* or *Rodriga* gave its name to the courtyard near Cannaregio, the only one with an independent well. There are also courtyards and lanes called *Mocato* and *Tubì* recorded in land registers, but these have been subsequently renamed. This provides undisputable confirmation of a further way in which the Sephardic group in Venice succeeded in manifesting their power and prestige. No Ashkenazi Jew achieved as much in the Campo di Ghetto Nuovo.

79

The central junction of the Ghetto Vecchio street network and the heart of its entire life was without doubt the *Campiello del Pozzo,* which became the *Campiello delle Scuole* after the two great Sephardic synagogues were built there. Its paving is punctuated by a white line, and in the centre is a well — one of only four in the entire Jewish quarter. Less sophisticated and less ornate than the one in Campo di Ghetto Nuovo, it consists of a round base in Istrian stone and a very simple well-head in Verona marble. The decoration, although in no specific style, suggests a 17th century dating, in any case earlier than the Scola Levantina extension of the 1680s, which upset the symmetry of the Campiello.

Round about are the imposing façades of the two synagogues and, at opposite sides, the two "skyscrapers" one of which is seven storeys high, creating a sense of shut-in suffocation because of disproportion between the buildings' base area and height — very

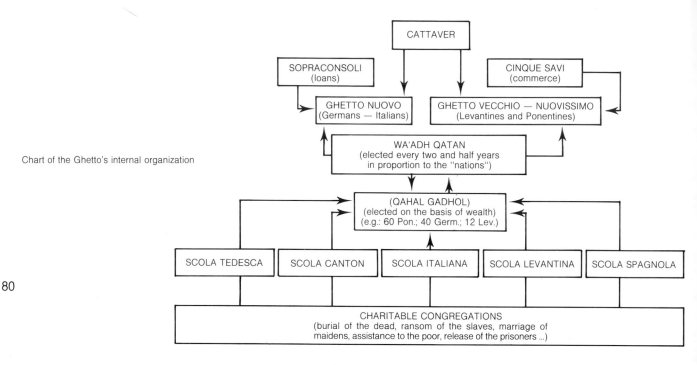

Chart of the Ghetto's internal organization

CATTAVER

SOPRACONSOLI
(loans)

CINQUE SAVI
(commerce)

GHETTO NUOVO
(Germans — Italians)

GHETTO VECCHIO — NUOVISSIMO
(Levantines and Ponentines)

WA'ADH QATAN
(elected every two and half years
in proportion to the "nations")

(QAHAL GADHOL)
(elected on the basis of wealth)
(e.g.: 60 Pon.; 40 Germ.; 12 Lev.)

SCOLA TEDESCA SCOLA CANTON SCOLA ITALIANA SCOLA LEVANTINA SCOLA SPAGNOLA

CHARITABLE CONGREGATIONS
(burial of the dead, ransom of the slaves, marriage of
maidens, assistance to the poor, release of the prisoners ...)

80

The overall consolidation achieved by the Jewish quarter by the end of the 16th century, with three "nations" German, Levantine and Ponentine officially recognized within the *Università,* led also to the perfecting of the organization and administration of the entire community, exhibiting a conspicuous ambition on the part of the Ghetto leaders to win themselves a guaranteed liberty in the matter of internal jurisdiction. The "Università's" *Libro Grande,* part of which was translated into Italian in the 17th century, is the explicit expression of such a determination. It consists of a series of statutes which governed the life of the quarter — some say, as if to make it a "republic within the Republic" — their application sometimes involving the harshest of spiritual punishments, *ḥerem* (excommunication). Their determination was so marked that it inevitably faced the Venetian authorities with the problem of whether or not it was justifiable to concede such independence to foreign groups living in the city. The dispute on this matter which arose in the early 17th

century between the Councillors of the Republic consisted, on the one side, of asserting the sovereignty of the State not just over single individuals but over an entire group, and on the other, of respecting the institutions of a community with its own rich tradition of laws and regulations which could not be utterly wiped out just because they were living under conditions of segregation.

The few documents available do not permit the reconstruction of their entire bureaucratic hierarchy with absolute certainty, nor do they clarify the effective relationships between the various elements in the structure, but it is nevertheless possible to identify certain precise links between the internal authorities and the State officials who controlled the various sectors of the Ghetto, which affords an adequate indication of the overall organization.

Until the early 18th century, when the *Inquisitorato sopra gli Ebrei* (Jewish Inquiry Board) was favoured together with other lesser magistratures, it was mainly the *Cattaveri* who supervised

the internal administration of the Ghetto Nuovo and the external administration of the entire Ghetto, always turning down requests from the *Cinque Savi alla Mercanzia,* who controlled activities inside the Ghetto Vecchio, for possession of the Ghetto Vecchio keys. Only in the delicate matter of loans were the *Sopraconsoli* involved, while the Ghetto, conceived as a community organization, was represented outside by a lesser council (*wa'adh qatan*) and run internally by a general assembly (*qahal gadhol*) elected on the basis of wealth and therefore with a Sephardic majority. Below this were the administrators for the internal affairs of every individual synagogue or community distinguished by a particular liturgical ritual (*qahal qadhosh*), while below these individual congregations lay the companies or *Confraternite* which were formed for charitable, religious and humanitarian purposes and often inspired by repeated mystic and cabalistic infiltration. It was indeed a city within a city.

According to the precept of Abraham in *Genesis* XVII, 11-12, every male child must de circumcised when he is eight days old, his health permitting. The event is a fundamental episode in a Jew's life. After the parents have chosen "a godfather who must hold the child while he is being circumcised and a godmother who fetches him from his house ... and the circumcisor who is called *Mohel* ... " they hold a prayer watch. "In the morning two Chairs with silken cushions are prepared in the School, or in their own house if they want to circumcise him there, one for the Godfather, who sits there to hold the boy while he is being circumcised, the

other, some say, for Elijah the Prophet, who they believe is present, always invisible, at every Circumcision, having been jealous of the observation of Israel's covenant, as in the Rules in Chapter 3. And many people gather, and the Circumcisor comes with a plate on which are his instruments and necessary things such as razor, stemming powder, swabs with oil of roses, and some like to prepare also a bowl of sand to dispose of the foreskin when it is cut off, and some Hymns are sung when the Godmother arrives with the boy in her arms, with an assembly of women, and at the temple door she hands him to the Godfather, and then

all those present cry *Baruch Abà*, which means Welcome. The Godfather sits down on his Chair and takes the boy and sets him on his knee, the Circumcisor unswaddles him, ... takes the razor, and says *Blessed be thou o Lord, and he whose circumcision thou hast commanded*, and cuts ... then places Dragon's oil on the cut, and coral powder, and things that stem the bleeding, and swabs with oil of roses, and binds it tightly, and swaddles him". (Leon Modena, *Historia de' riti hebraici*, Calleoni, Venice 1638, f.95-96.)

Venice - Museum of Jewish Art: The ceremony of *milah* (cicumcision), illustration with a greetings message by M.G. Gallico, gift of G. Malta (late 18th C.)

"In greatest veneration above all other Feasts, the Jews keep the Sabbath day ... commanded since the start of creation, in Genesis in the 2nd Chapter and twice in the Decalogue and many other places. Where is then declared that it is prohibited to do any work, and to rest." (Leon Modena, *Historia...,* f.56.) On Friday evening the rabbis or their deputies patrol the streets and lanes to see that the shops are closed, and exhort people to light the Sabbath lamps. In the middle of the Ghetto, a non-Jew paid by the community (the Sabbath trumpeter) sounded his trumpet two hours before the beginning of the feast, three times, at half-hourly intervals, to give warning to all to cease any work or commercial activity. "When comes, therefore, the 23rd hour of Friday, about half an hour before sunset, it is understood that the Feast has begun, with all the decreed prohibitions. And each woman is expected to light an oil lamp in the house, with at least four or six wicks, to last a great part of the night. And they prepare the table with a white cloth and bread, and over the bread another long narrow cloth that covers it; they say in memory of the Manna, which fell thus covered below, and above with dew and on the Sabbath it rained not." (Leon Modena, *Historia...,* f.59.)

82

The lighting of the Sabbath lamp (18th C. print)

Portuguese nuptial ceremony, from *Religious Ceremonies and Customs* by B. Picart (1733); print taken from A. Novelli and engraved on copper by A. Baratti (Venice 1789)

"Every Jew is obliged to take a wife ... firstly that he may beget children, as God says unto Adam in Genesis at the beginning ... to have at least one male child and one female, as then they intended to carry out this precept ..." (Leon Modena, *Historia...,* f.83). When the marriage is arranged, after having drawn up the marriage contract (*Kethubbah*) and after a period of betrothal, "when the time arrives for the wedding, and the day is named, which is customarily while the moon is waxing, on Wednesday or Friday for maidens and on Thursday for widows" and after the bride has taken her ritual bath on the evening before the ceremony, "at the time desired, the bridal couple are conducted into a hall or room, under a canopy, with music, and some have a number of boys standing by, holding lighted torches and singing. The people being gathered from round about, a square mantle with pendant charms, called *Taléd*, is placed to cover the heads of the bride and groom together. The Rabbi of the place, or the School's Cantor, or the closest relative, having taken a cup or carafe of wine in his hand, says a blessing to God; Who has created man and woman and ordained matrimony, and so on, and he gives the groom and the bride the wine to drink. Then the groom places the ring on her finger in the presence of two witnesses, who are usually the Rabbis, saying to her, now you are wedded to me, according to the Rite of Moses and Israel. They read the dowry card, in which for the dowry received the groom binds himself to feed her and stay with her, etc, and they receive his undertaking. And then with another vase of wine they sing six more benedictions, seven in all, and give both the spouses more to drink, and pour wine on the ground as a sign of merrymaking, and when the vase is empty it is handed to the groom, who dashes it to the ground and breaks it, to remind himself, while merrymaking, of death, which breaks us and shatters us as glass, that he shall not be puffed up. And then all the people cry *Mazal tov*, which means, be of good fortune, and they go away." (Leon Modena, *Historia...,* f.86.)

The death of a Ghetto inhabitant involved (and still does) a whole series of particularly significant ritual acts.

"When the spirit has been yielded up, they place the body in the ground, wrapped in a shroud, with the face covered and a wax candle at the head" Leon Modena recounts in his *Historia...*, f.107.

Then funeral conveyance came about, organized by a "company" which existed within every "nation" and supervised all activities linked to the event. Leaving from Cannaregio, the boat traditionally followed a course which passed first through the open lagoon, then under the bridge of San Pietro di Castello, and arrived finally at the Lido. Only from the mid 17th century, because of the continual insults that the funeral corteges suffered from the common people when they passed under the bridge, the course was changed to pass round outside, on the lagoon, until it landed at San Nicolò,

where each "nation" had its own separate burial ground.

"So they take it to the place of burial, which is a whole field set aside for this custom, which they call *Bet Achaim*, meaning House of the Living, saying that the dead are alive in spirit, somebody there gives a sermon full of his praises, then an orison is said, beginning with the words from *Deuteronomy* ch.32: *Dei perfecta sunt opera, et omnes viae eius iudicia* (God's work is perfect, for all his ways are judgment). Having said *Zidduch addin*, placed a sack of earth beneath the head and nailed down the coffin, they carry it to the grave, which is a hole already dug to size, procured so as to be near other dead relatives. In some places they place the coffin there beside the grave, but only for men, then ten people circle the coffin seven times saying an orison for the soul of the dead, but others do not do this. And the dead person's next of kin rends his own garment some-

what, then they lower him into the grave, and cover him with earth, each person throwing in a spadeful or a handful of earth, until it is covered." (Leon Modena *Historia...*, f.108.)

Burial of an Ashkenazi Jew, anonymous 18th C. painting on wood

Venice - Museum of Jewish Art: Case for the Scrolls of the Law (*tiq*), gift of Family Lewi (17th-18th C.)

only the Sephardic merchants were to any extent able to fill. The opportunity offered to the inhabitants of the Ghetto Vecchio to avail themselves, for trade purposes, of good contacts with the oriental communities, and in this way to obviate, often, the gross risks inherent in maritime commerce, enabled them not only to consolidate an already flourishing position but also to extend their field of action into hitherto untried areas. Nor could interference by the *Cattaver* magistrates in their internal affairs hinder them from re-establishing long-interrupted links with North Africa, Tunis and Algiers in particular, on the suggestion of Moisè Yisra'el and Dawidh Navarro in 1622. A memorandum of 15 March 1625 from the *Cinque Savi* acknowledged that the particular growth in trade had been due to the contribution of Sephardic and Levantine families and ascribed to them the main credit for traffic with the East after the opening of the port of Spalato (Split), calculating the Jewish contribution to the public good and the city's private use to be as much as 100,000 ducats a year in good currency. It is therefore not surprising that the economic expansion of the Ghetto Vecchio inhabitants was scarcely impeded either by the heavy taxation imposed on them or by the contribution they were unwillingly but ever more relentlessly obliged to pay, between 1598 and 1611, towards the running of the pawn shops, in order to alleviate the Germans' onerous burden (although the wayfarers and the Corfioti (from Corfu) were exempted). Actually, the increase in the jewel trade, in spite of arguments and opposition from Venetian persons of authority, enabled them to accumulate fresh capital and win a role that even Simone Luzzatto, one of the foremost rabbis of the age, recognized in his explanatory *Discorso* as essential to the "illustrious city of Venice". When, therefore, in 1639, after the renewed *condotta* of 10 July 1636 had confirmed all earlier privileges, the *Cinque Savi* finally granted them permission to stay outside the Ghetto, even during forbidden hours, so as not to compromise the development of business affairs, that

The first decade of the 17th century is considered by modern historians to be the period of greatest stability in the long story of the Venetian Ghetto from all points of view, economic, social, cultural and religious.

There had been internal friction between individual ethnic groups, since a predominantly Ashkenazi community had had to change within a very short time to one with a Sephardic (Ponentine) majority, also within one "nation" itself, between Levantine wayfarers and residents, but all this was eventually smoothed out, and inside the area of segregation the worst contrasts and inequalities were modified and a balance was achieved, fragile, but never again to be upset.

Firstly, the Sephardic "nation" consolidated its commercial reputation and

its wealth, acquiring more and more weight within the Venetian economy. The Levantines had suffered internal disputes arising after the death of Daniel Rodriga, but managed to settle them with the *condizione* signed in 1604, and subsequently seem to have reaped some indirect advantage, together with the Sephardim, from the unstable conditions affecting *La Serenissima*. In fact, with the gradual shift of the commercial axis towards the Atlantic, the Republic was losing its dominion over the Mediterranean and its slow decline had begun. At the same time, the Venetian aristocracy, also involved in internal struggles and a dispute with the Church, was decidedly changing into a landed aristocracy, abdicating its role as a merchant class and leaving a vacuum in the Adriatic economy that

privilege was only a way of recognizing, indirectly, that their valuable presence was now essential.

In addition, even the Ghetto Nuovo Ashkenazim were able to benefit, though slowly and to a reduced extent, from a period of greater stability and economic security. Always limited in their working opportunities and tied to the already static difficulties of the credit market, they had sought the road towards a less strict limitation of their activities in a justifiable desire to emulate the Sephardim and tap more profitable commercial sectors. An early gleam on their dark horizon was provided by the involvement of the Levantine residents and the Sephardim, together with some communities from the mainland, in the maintenance of the "poverty banks". Their participation somewhat alleviated the economic stranglehold on the San Girolamo quarter, permitting initiatives in other directions. In spite of slight differences like a trading concession to Germans with sufficient capital, the *condotta* renewals in 1618, 1624 and 1629, with their detailed, close-written paragraphs framed to regulate the life of the banks or to confirm exclusion from certain crafts and professions such as tailoring and printing, had in effect continued to sanction a state of discrimination with regard to Levantine and Ponentine privileges. Nevertheless in the 1630s the Germans were able to "supplicate" the State to obtain concessions designed to improve their internal conditions. On 29 December 1634, the Senate, although reconfirming previous *condottas* both on general lines and in details, went so far as to respond positively to a request in this sense, allowing the Ashkenazim to participate, in a limited way, in the maritime trade until then reserved only for the inhabitants of the Ghetto Vecchio. "The *Cinque Savi alla Mercanzia* can and must concede to the German Jews the trade with the Levant" runs the text of the agreement, in part at least healing a disparity which in time would certainly have brought harmful consequences to Ghetto life. And, as evidence of the new goodwill towards the oldest "nation" in the Jewish quarter, it

added permission for revision on those books which it might be necessary "to have printed for their ritual" thus lifting a ban that had previously been several times re-endorsed.

These were, admittedly, only fractional gains that could do little to reduce the disparities between the "nations" but all the same they were steps in the right direction, partly mitigating the more glaring frictions and guaranteeing for everyone a sufficiently stable if not very high standard of living.

This happy condition, although really quite flimsy, even induced an illusion of well-being in many people, to the extent that there seems to have been some motive for the many injunctions designed to restrain ostentatious luxury and pomp issued by the Ghetto leaders in 1616 — the elegance of Jewish women seemed to Thomas Coryat inferior only to that of English countesses — or that of 1628 against the spread of gambling, for, behind the appearance of opulence, they were acutely aware of the undisputable signs of possible imminent decadence. Yet for the moment, in

relation to such situations, the Ghetto at that time enjoyed the greatest demographic development ever recorded throughout the centuries of the Venetian Diaspora. The steady increase could not be arrested either by the tragic episodes of the 1630-31 plague, though it claimed many victims within the Jewish community, nor by the temporary economic standstill that followed it. Instead it contributed, through the indefatigable Sephardic initiative, to the opening in 1633 of a third sector of the Ghetto, the Nuovissimo Ghetto, (Newest Ghetto) whose lanes and more decorous palaces were able to accommodate some of the Jewish quarter's most reputable families, attracted back to Venice by the new situation. Although it is hard to credit the population figure of 6,000 suggested by Simone Luzzatto in his *Discorso* (f.28 r.) when describing the situation in the early 17th century, it is reasonably certain that there were at least 4,500 Jews living in the Ghettos then, the greatest number being Ashkenazim, and the most wealthy, without doubt, Sephardim.

86

כתובים

תהלים משלי איוב דניאל

עזרא ודברי הימים:

יצאו נצבים פתח אהליכם לזכות אתכם
בלכם היום׃

[Hebrew commentary text]

בויניציאה

Cō licétia de' Sup.

Kethubhim (hagiography) with a commentary by Rashi (Psalms, Proverbs, Job, Daniel, Ezra, Chronicles), Giovanni Bragadin, in the house of Giovanni Di Gara, Venice 5367 (1607)

◀ Interior of a Jewish School

In counterpart to the situation described, the segregated quarter also went through one of its most involved and flourishing cultural periods in the early 17th century, characterized by a busy intellectual life in a rare concentration of works and ideas, fertile exchanges between the Jewish intelligentsia and representatives of contemporary cultured society, and a vast and thriving literary production in both Hebrew and Italian, which may not have achieved artistic pinnacles but is of fundamental documentary interest and sometimes essential historical importance. The presence of many rabbis of high reputation — though divided between the conservative Halakhic orthodoxy of men like Shemu'el Aboaf and Azariah Figo and the moderate restorative of Leon Modena and Simone Luzzatto — and of particularly gifted personalities like the poetess Sara Copio Sullam, succeeded in making the Venetian scene a veritable reference point for all the western Diaspora, good enough to rival more famous centres such as Amsterdam for European primacy in doctrinal and religious matters. The restlessness typical of an age worried about the development of rigorous orthodoxy, alongside theories verging on hetero-

doxy, and inspired by messianic expectations and cabalistic motivations, was successfully contained, thanks to strict dedication, within dimensions capable of reconciling the ideological arguments and religious divergences and restoring to the entire Ghetto an authentic image of unity and stability. A practical sign of the determinaton to keep the old tradition alive as regards ritual and the interpretation of sacred texts was the opening in 1605 of a boarding school at Conegliano Veneto, subsidized by the community itself. Founded by Yiśra'el Conegliano and Dawidh Marcaria, entrusted to Nathan Ottolenghi and maintained by the diligence of Shim'on Copio (father of the poetess Sara), it was open to all young Italian students. The same year Shim'on Copio signed a circular which was sent to all the European communities asking for donations to the institution in order to perpetuate Biblical and rabbinical studies, presenting his request as a means of compensating for the "heavy yoke imposed" by the State. The positive situation was equally marked by the continuing recovery of the Hebrew press, on subjects concerning Jewish culture moreover. Besides the reissue of the famous Ashkenazic *maḥazor*, the Bible and the major commentaries, it is worth mentioning the publication of Biblical dictionaries (notably Leon Modena's *Galuth Yehudhah*, Sarzina, Venice, 1612) and also the interest of intellectuals in Italian translations of Jewish works (notably the translation of Mosheh da Rieti's *Little Sanctuary* by the Roman poetess Debhorah Ascarelli, published by Zanetti in 1601) and works written in Italian by Jewish authors (Leon Modena was involved in the publication of Angelo Alatini's *I Trionfi* by the Eredi del Salicato in 1611) by way of showing an interest in the world outside the Ghetto and its lay culture. Even though these publications in no case achieved the "*cinquecentine*" distinction, Di Gara and the Bragadina Press did further outstanding work until the new Vendramina Press appeared in 1631, destined to accompany the Bragadina itself into the second half of the 18th century.

In a period characterized by multiple, sometimes disquieting tendencies, one of the features that best expresses both the desire to emulate the Venetian intellectuals — as if to obtain, at least on the cultural level, the equality otherwise denied on the level of common rights — and the psychological craving to compensate for the state of segregation by developing the spiritual dimension, study in particular, was the literary salon of Sara Copio Sullam. She was certainly the most famous poetess in the whole history of Jewish Italian literature and her salon was a centre of attraction for many scholars, Jewish and others, a place for doctrinal and theological discussions and poetical debates. In its intellectual pattern it represents the concrete manifestation not only of a young woman's desire for poetical fame and glory — daughter as she was of one of the most eminent families in the Jewish quarter, her father being that Shim'on Copio who was actively engaged in the community's cultural resurgence — but also, more profoundly, of the flexible, two-way relationship between the Ghetto and the outside world, signifying, notwithstanding the tensions created by the counter-reformatory spirit, initiatives towards the "lay" world not to be found on such a scale at other times in the Jews' Venetian story.

Sara Copio was educated from girlhood in religious studies no less than in the reading of Italian and Latin classics, and married at the age of twenty to Ya'aqobh Sullam. Gifted with a good intellect and uncommon poetic abilities, she decided to break the circle of isolation and segregation and acquire wide literary fame by receiving the intellectual flower of Venice in her own home and making contact with scholars working outside the region. Ironically, the eccentricity of certain biographical incidents eventually made her more famous than her small output of poetry did. Reading the poem *La reina Ester* by the Genoese Ansaldo Cebà induced her to write to him, and their ensuing correspondence soon became a veritable literary exercise for him, on the lines of a sublimated Petrarchan style, in

which the affair of "love at a distance" for the "beautiful Jewess" led him so far as to attempt to convert his correspondent by constantly praising Christianity above the Jewish faith. Sara's heroic resistance, aided and abetted by the famous Leon Modena and her teacher Numidio Paluzzi, showed the same moral fibre and the same firm consistency that she demonstrated in 1621 when undertaking her own defence against the accusation of not believing in the immortality of the soul levelled at her by the Bishop of Capodistria, Baldassar Bonifacio, one of the frequenters of her salon.

This unfounded suspicion threatened dangerous consequences not only for herself but for the entire community, and the *Manifesto* she published to demolish it, adopting first a sarcastic

and denigratory tone towards her adversary, then becoming severe and resolute in the demonstration of her own theory, was an act of forceful steadfastness on the part of one who, fortified with truth, succeeded in finding a suitable defence in her own culture and her own conscience. It stands also as a reasoned defence of Judaism, all the more courageous for being delivered at a time of particular tension and difficulty. The poetess demonstrated equal resolution when, shamefully cheated and robbed, with vague accusations of witchcraft, by her own teacher assisted by some women of low morality, she had the sense to ask and indeed received justice from the law and from the literary world which, according to a *Ragguaglio* in Giulia Soliga's manuscript, ranged itself solidly behind her.

MANIFESTO
DI
SARRA COPIA
SVLAM HEBREA.

Nel quale è da lei riprouata, e detestata l'opinione negante l'immortalità dell'Anima, falsamente attribuitale dal

SIG. BALDASSARE BONIFACCIO.

Con Licenza de' Superiori.

IN VENETIA, M. DCXXI.
Appresso Giouanni Alberti.

In contrast, Sara's poetical vein wins scant recognition in her critical legacy, yet it cannot have been minor considering that her fame among contemporary scholars was considerable and widespread. Actually, all those who took an interest in her affairs and her small surviving output always praised her heroic resistance to every religious attack and her vigorous defence of Jewish tradition and faith; they sang her beauty and her moral virtues, but never expressed a considered opinion of her verses. Even Leon Modena, who was close to her and dedicated his tragedy *Ester* to her, seems almost obsequious in his praise of her brains and qualities of humility and compassion, but about her poetry he does not express any judgement beyond the recognition of an honest amateurish exercise.

Even the inscription on her tombstone, which the rabbi composed, appears to confirm this clearly: "*This is the tombstone of the distinguished / Signora Sara, wife of the living / Jacob Sullam / The angel of death hurled his dart mortally wounding Sara / a woman of high intelligence / Wise among wives, a support to the wretched / The poor man found in her a companion and friend / Though now she is consigned without mercy to the worms of the earth, on the day / appointed the Lord will say: Return, return O Shulamite / Died on the sixth day (Friday) 5 'adhar 5401 (1641) / may her soul enjoy eternal bliss*".

The impossibility of forming a judgement on such a small output — of occasional verse moreover — does not diminish our duty to recognize the historical value of her cultural presence and evaluate the importance of an existence that transcends the particular case to become emblematic of a situation and a determination to succeed that can be sincerely appreciated.

מצבת קבורת הצנועה מרת ש ר ה אשת כמ׳
יעקב סולם יצ״ו:

ירה בחין	מלאך לוחין
הטיר המית:	שרת טעם
נזר רשים	הכמת נשים
חבר עמית:	אצלה כל דל
בלתי פדיום	אם היא כיום
עש וסמית:	תקות רמה
יאמר האל	עת בוא גואל
הסולמית	שובי שובי
נפטרה יום ו׳ ה׳ אדר הת״א:	

Venice - Old Jewish Cemetery on San Nicolò di Lido: Grave of Sara Copio Sullam (1590?-1641) and text of her gravestone

◀ Title page of the *Manifesto* by Sara Copio Sullam, published in Venice in 1621 by Alberti and Pinelli

The man who, in other ways, succeeded in focussing on himself the attention of the entire Ghetto and many intellectuals outside it and, at the same time, dominating the various aspects of religious and social life in the Jewish quarter with his own cultural eclecticism was Leon Modena (1571-1648), perhaps the most discussed and controversial character, and certainly the best known, in the entire history of the Venetian community. Different, in fact, from other leading figures whose particulars still escape us, he left an *Autobiografia* (The Life of Judas), which in spite of the inevitable intrusions due to the particular literary genre, provides the clearest access to a factual knowledge of his life and culture. In effect, the profile he draws of himself goes beyond the mere chronicle of the facts of an eventful and at times adventurous life. Although constructed in conventional form, praising the greatness and justice of God, to whose will man is always subject, sustained by unshakeable faith, it captures highly revealing traits of character. For one thing, it is a constant celebration of himself, his precociousness in reading and in interpreting the scriptures, his ability in preaching, filling the synagogue with a huge congregation, many of them not Jewish, his many-sided interests — he lists a good 26 professions! — and the wide variety of fields on which he left the mark of his own superior talents. In contrast, with a sort of *voluptas dolendi*, he continually wallows in self commiseration, enumerating the many disasters that beset his life, from the murder of his beloved son to his insane passion for gambling and the constant struggle against poverty that negated everything he tried. His only resources, which never deserted him and always helped him to resolve unnerving situations, were intelligence and culture, religious and secular, covering the most disparate interests in an inexhaustible thirst for knowledge.

These were the powers that enabled Leon Modena to produce highly demanding texts, associating useful discussion on certain aspects of Talmudism with defence against outside attacks or Cabalistic interferences — though he followed them in his youth. They also enabled him, with an ever-ready response, to assume positions on delicate doctrinal or theological questions, to welcome the dominant fashion for baroque poetry, reworking the tragedy *Ester* by S. Usque and publishing the pastoral play *I Trionfi* by Angelo Alatini, composing the now lost *Rachele e Giacobbe*, and making his own essential contribution to the spread of choral singing against opposition from the orthodox wing of Venetian rabbis. In 1628 he in fact directed the *Music Academy* founded in the Ghetto by a group of immigrants from Mantua and known as the *Accademia degli Imperiti*, or by a verse from the Bible, *Bezokhrenu 'eth-tziyon* (By the waters of Babylon we sat down and wept — *Psalm* CXXXVII, 1). He was concerned,

lastly, with popular but high quality texts such as the Biblical dictionary (*Galuth Yehudhah*) and the *Historia de' riti hebraici*, intended to make known the customs and rituals of the Israelite religion. Voluble and many-sided as he was, but always earning admiration for his qualities, his name soon spread beyond the confines of the Ghetto, his famous reputation introducing him to Jewish scholars or Christian Hebraists with whom he conducted an ample correspondence. He was the true catalyst of the Ghetto's fervid activity, capable of reflecting in himself all the anxieties of a society constrained to live in a state of subjection, together with the internal contradictions of a spirituality distracted in difficult times by disruptive forces. He was capable of attacking oral tradition and Talmudic Judaism, yet skilful in mediating be-

HISTORIA
DE RITI HEBRAICI
Vita & osseruanze degl'
Hebrei di questi tempi
DI
LEON MODENA RABI H.°
Da Venetia
Gia stampata in Parigi
& hora da lui corretta e
riformata
Con licenza de Superiori
IN VENETIA 1638.
Appresso Gia Calleoni

Traditional portrait of Leon Modena from *Historia de' riti hebraici*, Calleoni, Venice 1638

Title page of Leon Modena's *Historia de' riti hebraici*, Calleoni, Venice 1638

tween the old and the new, even with ideological swings, and sometimes in welcoming schemes consonant with the age without ever abandoning his respect for Halakhic standards set by the elders.

Leon Modena sometimes pursued his manifold interests and cultural eclecticism at the expense of original investigation, and here and there created a certain dissipation which involved scholars, mainly from the 19th century (Reggio, Geiger, Libowitz, etc) and some from the 20th (Rivkin), in trying to recover a doctrinal coherence which may ocasionally appear compromised. It is nonetheless undeniable that he never lost sight of two constant commitments: firstly, the intention to spread the true substance of the Jewish faith to an outside public, convinced that only an authentic knowledge devoid of deliberate distortions or preconceptions could ensure healthy relations and the advantages of reciprocal respect between the religions; secondly, the determination to discuss traditional Judaism from moderate positions within it, while firmly defending it from outside attack, armed with an extraordinary mastery of texts from various sources and a remarkably acute intellectual curiosity. The second objective crystallized into Hebrew works designed for a limited public but widely influential, such as *Sha'aghath 'aryeh* (The Roar of the Lion) — written to confute the violent attack on rabbinical tradition contained in the anonymous *Qol sakhal* (The Voice of the Fool), attributed by some to Modena himself as a reflection of his reforming phase, which he later got over — and *Maghen wetzinnah* (Shield and Defence), compiled on an official commission from the Jewish *Università* to combat the dangerous heretical texts sent by Uriel da Costa to the Venetian community in 1616, also a vigorous *Diffesa* (1627), written against attacks on the *Talmudh* moved by Brother Sisto Senese, who accused the text of immorality and anti-Christian spirit. The first objective — to explain the Jewish faith to the world at large — strengthened by the open-minded attitude he had already woven into certain arguments in

91

the *Diffesa*, led Modena to compose perhaps the most coherent and complete explanation of Hebrew rituals and beliefs up to then written for a non-Jewish public, beyond all religious barriers and ideological prejudices, the *Historia de' riti hebraici*. Written in the years 1616-17 with the intention "to inform, not to persuade" in order to gratify the curiosity of certain Christian intellectuals, it was published in 1637 in Paris, unknown to the author, by the Frenchman Jacques Gaffarel. He broke the news to Modena in a letter, throwing him into immediate panic. The awareness that the text contained some statements that could certainly have caused the censor to intervene drove him to present himself spontaneously at the *Sant'Uffizio* and declare his readiness to eliminate whatever passages might seem offensive to the Christian faith and change any sentence that might be suspect. The reply from Brother Marco Ferro justified his apprehensions, enjoining him to cut certain statements principally regarding the articles of faith, the reincarnation and the immateriality of God. When Modena finally saw the Paris edition, however, he found with surprised relief that these doctrinal passages had been removed from his original by his prudent French friend. A revised and expurgated edition of the *Historia* appeared in Venice in 1638, initiating a fortunate progress which, in spite of some quite bitter criticism from 19th century German historians, would continue for centuries. The clear, coherent picture of Jewish custom and usage traced by Modena with the sole aim of "helping the public and defending my own much depressed nation" could in fact boast several translations, and was described as the most complete and well organized presentation of the life of Israel, usable on various levels as a reliable book of reference.

92

The Venetian Ghetto's most famous rabbi, by way of completing the self portrait he left in his *Autobiografia*, decided to portray his human side in his will, so as to hand on to his heirs his genuine interior qualities, aside from the inconsistencies and anxieties of a life not devoid of contradictions and fluctuating, confusing vicissitudes. Alluding to

his own funeral eulogy, he recommends that they should avoid excessive praise and say "that I was not one of the hypocrites; my inside is like my outside; I have walked in the fear of the Lord, and kept away from evil more in private than in public, and have never had regard for a friend or a relative or even myself, or for anything that might have been useful to me when it concerned what I thought was the truth; I have been kind to people both great and small". No less revealing are his instructions for a simple funeral service, accompanied by the singing of only one psalm, and his burial in the San Nicolò cemetery. The man who had composed, in lucid, solemn Hebrew, the most

sophisticated funerary inscriptions for the most eminent persons of his time asked to lie beside his mother and his own children under a very simple stone bearing the most modest words, which reflected the true greatness of the man: "*The departed sayeth: they have acquired Judas Leon Modena above — be gentle with him and give him peace — six feet of earth in this enclosure as an eternal possession*". He died on the Sabbath, 27 *'adhar* 5408 — 21 March 1648.

Venice - Old Jewish Cemetery on San Nicolò di Lido: Tomb of Leon Modena

Venice - Old Jewish Cemetery on San Nicolò di Lido: Stone marking the common grave of plague victims 1630-31

16th C. amulet against the plague, with Cabalistic formulas and symbols mixed with non-Hebrew elements; from the *Sha 'ar ha-yihudh* by H. Vital

All commercial activity and cultural fervour suffered a brusque interruption when the Ghetto too was struck by the terrible plague that spread throughout Europe in 1630-31. Their strict isolation and the standards of hygiene that Jews adhered to for religious reasons had the effect only of retarding the contagion, and despite many preventive measures it became rampant in the Jewish quarter from the late summer of 1630 to the end of October 1631. The treatment suggested by the doctor Yehoshua' Chabiglio and his concern to fetch twelve experts to the city to control the shocking situation proved of no avail. Leon Modena recounts in his *Autobiografia* that the plague "reached here, Venice, after starting during the days of atonement in the Ghetto Vecchio with the late lamented Signor Mosè Sarfatti and in the days of Sukkoth with Signor Giacobbe Kohen known as Schicco; and it has spread so much that up to now, the first of *'iyyar* 5391 (1631), 170 people have died. This brought much

confusion in the community and many, especially the Sephardim, have gone from the city towards the east or towards Verona. Great riches, 750 parcels, were sent to the Lazaret and nearly everything has been ruined, spoiled and lost. For about a year Jews have been forbidden to buy, sell or trade, and therefore nothing has been earned; furthermore, the government has taken over 120 thousand ducats from the Jews. The shortage of everything is worse than it has ever been, so that the Israelites of this community are impoverished and made wretched, the rich have sunk to the level of the middle class, those of the middle class have become poor, and the poor have no one to take pity on them because the money is finished". Every religious institution was offering up prayers for the contagion to cease. Some despaired when they saw their own houses surrounded by death, while others, terrified, fled before human impotence. The young Benedetto Luzzatto, a disciple of

Modena's, having lost the woman he loved, "to relieve his oppressed mind somewhat" and escape from "the travail of the contagious evil" sought diversion in literary fantasy, in the "ideal Arcady" created in his pastoral play *L'amor possente*. The plague mowed down quite a large number of victims; chronicles and documents of the time permit an estimate of about 450 people, whose death, taking into account the great number of merchants who managed to leave the Ghetto, meant a steep decline in the population and an unprecedented economic crisis. The emergency situation obliged the leaders of the community to adopt exceptional measures, among which was the necessary choice of common burial, commemorated today by a rough-hewn gravestone in the cemetery at San Nicolò bearing the stark inscription "Hebrei 1631". The terrible scourge came to an end only in the final months of 1631, leaving the city decimated and the Ghetto in a state of prostration that only a strenuous determination to recover was able to alleviate.

The end of the contagion was celebrated in the Ghetto synagogues by special public ceremonies preceded by penitential fasting, and votive offerings were made to mark their recovery from the nightmare. At the same time, the Jews commemorated their liberation from the epidemic by an event of lasting importance, the opening in the Ghetto Nuovo of a new Scola-midhrash belonging to the Ashkenazi ritual — the *Scola Mesullamim*. According to a note in an old book belonging to the Scola Canton (Ottolenghi), although it is true that nobody "knows the time it was opened or by whom or for what cause; it is however supposed that it was started at the time the plague struck Venice, in 1680".

It seems to be a case of the wrong date, and a persistent theory suggests that it meant in fact to refer to 1630. As the theory seems likely, it can be presumed that a certain Mosheh Mesullam Lewi mentioned in the preface to the German *maḥazor* published in the 17th century, either to propitiate divine grace or as an act of thanksgiving for recovery from the plague sickness, opened the small place of worship and study (now unfortunately vanished) near the Agudi bridge on the west side of the *Campo*. Of course its decorative features and its interior structure are unknown, and nothing remains of its constituent elements except for a *Sepher* (Scroll of the Law) inherited from the German synagogue in Padua, the 18th century manuscript book that lay in the Scola Canton until the Second World War (Ottolenghi), printed lists of benefactors, forms of prayer (including a benediction in memory of the famous doctor Salomone Ashkenazi, who played a great part in resolving the difficult relations between the Ghetto and the State in 1573), some internal orders and a brief Hebrew inscription, now almost illegible but connected with the alms box, probably from beside the old entrance door. Nevertheless a long-standing oral tradition, not actually documented, maintains that when, after 1840, the little hall was abandoned, "by

reason of the expense they had to meet because of the state it was in, although it was small" as the above-mentioned manuscript says in an added note, and the Scola's frequenters were welcomed by the Scola Grande Tedesca, the *'aron* was transported to the nearby *Casa di Industria* (later *di Ricovero* now *di Riposo*) *Israelitica* set up in 1844, where it adorns the little temple, the lower part of whose walls are wood panelled and the ceiling painted like a serene starry sky.

In stone, approached by steps and two Corinthian columns on high bases supporting a simple architrave with the crown motif in the centre, it is probably the only surviving element of the structures of the small *midhrash* that for two centuries housed the devotions and studies of a small group of Ashkenazi Jews. All the rest was completely lost when the building was demolished in 1896 (Morpurgo).

אנא נגילה נשמחה כלנו
בדהבות עיר הזאת כתוף ונבל
רב לך ויניציאה עוד רדוף האבל
הן כיעתה הרחיב צ׳ לנו
מקצה הארץ עד יצה הארץ
שלום ירבה קדוש וצור העיד

Venice - Ghetto Nuovo, Museum of Jewish Art: Inscription on leather, celebrating deliverance from a grave disaster

▶ Venice - Ghetto Nuovo: the 'aron from the Scola Mesullamim (?) now in the *Casa di Riposo Israeliti-ca*

It seems not unreasonable, however, to advance the hypothesis, though yet to be documented, that another relic, still surviving but in very poor condition, may in some way be connected to the little Ashkenazi prayer hall. In fact the Scola Mesullamim did perhaps own — and in that case very probably use for its inauguration — thirteen Hebrew inscriptions on leather which appear from a private document to have been re-used, together with many other pieces, to adorn the women's gallery in the Scola Italiana until 1929, then kept until 16 October 1940 in the home of the lawyer Giuseppe Grego, and deposited since then in the Scola Canton, where at least part of the material from the demolished little house of prayer had already been collected. Written on six lines which hold in acrostic the name of one 'Abhraham, while the last line always begins with the word *shalom* (is this just a coincidence with the 19th century inscriptions at the Scola Italiana?), they clearly refer, with Biblical quotations and poetic imagery, to the ending of a period of grave disaster and sickness, with a final exhortation to joy and faith in God, like the third: "Come, let us all be merry and rejoice; in the streets of the city with drums and cymbals; enough, enough, Venice, leave thy mourning, for now the Lord hath delivered us from evil; from one corner of the earth to the other, may the Saint make peace, defence and power to increase" while the eighth, celebrating the spiritual value of the recently built or rebuilt little prayer hall, runs: "Though this house that we have built has a low roof sloping to the street ... with the best things thou wilt adorn it: in it scholars shall understand the majesty and the grandeur of the Torah" followed at once in the ninth by a quotation from *Psalm XXX*, which is sung during the feast of *Ḥanukkah* in memory of the inauguration of the Temple, profaned by Antiochus Epiphanes, and traditionally recited when any new house or building is inaugurated, but also contains, however, the thanksgiving of an individual who seems to have been cured of a serious illness: "O Lord my God, I cried unto thee and thou hast healed me". Since at no point, as far as we know, does the Ghetto history record the coincidence of all these events, there is no choice but to suppose that all the inscriptions at present held by the Jewish Museum really do refer to the founding of the Scola Mesullamim, and that in them the donor is asking *shalom* (peace) for his own father 'Abhraham, as did Isacco Norza in the Scola Italiana in the early 19th century, perhaps reusing them for the women's gallery of his own synagogue and adding the decorative epigraphs — unless we decide to recognize in the fourth line of the third inscription (reproduced here) a not impossible indication of the date 5485 (1725) or 5505 (1745), in which case the inscriptions would remain a mystery, since up to now we know of no event that can be connected with such a date.

95

THE RECOVERY

The years immediately following that painful and harrowing episode were characterized by a determination for economic recovery and a revived cultural and religious drive — both constant factors in Ghetto life — which took the form of the opening of new prayer and study halls, the extension of the Ghetto boundary, and the compilation of works fundamental to the understanding of the actual quality of the Jewish presence in Venice.

There seems to have been no connection between the plague and the opening or re-establishment between the 16th and the 17th centuries of two more Ashkenazi *midhrashim* in the Ghetto Nuovo, the *Scola Kohanim* and the *Scola Luzzatto*. Rather, they were a reflection of the religious fervour and renewed devotion to scriptural study that characterized the early 17th century, also of the active presence in this context of private and personal variations within one and the same *minhagh* (ritual), sometimes originating in single family groups. The first of the schools, almost certainly founded by a family called Kohen, rose beside the portico leading to the bridge across to the Ghetto Nuovissimo, but when the building that housed it was partly demolished in 1893 all its movable furnishings and all the decorative fittings were transported to the *midhrash* open since 1733-36 on the left-hand side of the entrance lobby of the Scola Spagnola, which in that very year was undergoing the latest major restoration in its long existence. Given the process of adaptation to the surrounding Sephardic structure, its original overall appearance can in no way be reconstructed, although it is reasonable to suppose that it was fairly complex. A land register of 1739 states that above the Scola "of the men" there was another "for use by the women"; no other evidence remains, apart from a book now in the Jewish Museum, but a small inscription on wood reproducing the Sabbath evening prayer *'atah ḥonantanu ... — Thou hast granted us...*, preceded by the hands of the Kohen (priest) in the act of blessing; it was done in 1829 by one 'Eli-

96

'ezer Kohen Porto, and is now housed in the little temple of the *Casa di Riposo*, to the right of the 'aron.

The traditional demands of orientation have strongly governed the placing of the two focal points of the original hall in these rectangular surroundings with the entrance to the Scola Spagnola on the long wall. The simple wooden Ark of the Covenant surmounted by the Tablets of the Law, the pews for wor-shippers arranged crosswise, the lectern for the officiant placed opposite the 'aron on the long side in a very one-sided position in relation to the entrance, which is on the same side, preserve of the original layout only the sense of severe austerity.

Venice - Old Jewish Cemetery on San Nicolò di Lido: Kohanim's (priests) hands in the gesture of blessing on an old tombstone

Venice - Ghetto Vecchio: Scola Luzzatto, inside the Scola Levantina

now far from its original site. It was founded by the family of the same name, near the present bridge over the Rio di San Girolamo. Its overall layout and its decorative structures were carefully preserved when, in 1836, the building that housed it being destroyed, it was removed with all its trappings to the Scola Levantina and installed in the long rectangular room opening to the right off the entrance lobby. In conformity with the original bifocal layout, the new scheme places the *'aron* and the *bimah* facing each other, visually connected by wooden panelling and benches along the walls, interrupted only by the entrance which opens in the centre of a long side, opposite the four large rectangular windows and the doorway, now closed, which give onto the Campiello delle Scuole. A similar function is also performed by the worshippers' pews, arranged parallel to the long sides and leaving a space in the middle where the floor is paved with ordinary geometric tiles. The wooden Ark of the Covenant is framed by columns on high bases supporting a simple architrave with the Tablets of the Law, and surrounded by a 19th century balustrade. The *bimah*, very simple, is raised four steps above floor level, reminiscent of the Scola Canton and the Scola Italiana in the Ghetto Nuovo. The decoration, very sober and austere, is completed by a fine timbered ceiling, while in the panels on the upper part of the walls, conforming to a style to be seen in the Ghetto Nuovo halls, a series of inscriptions in Hebrew praise God and repeat, in acrostics, the name of 'Eliyyahu 'Aharon Ḥazaq. On the inside cornice of the glazed entrance door the inscription recites: "*Barukh 'atah be-bho'ekha ubarukh 'atah betze 'thekha — Blessed shalt thou be when thou comest in, and blessed shalt thou be when thou goest out*" (*Deuteronomy* XXVIII, 6), as if to confirm, in its echo of a verse from the Torah, the devotion to study and the dedication to the scriptures that have illuminated the little synagogue for centuries. During the 1950 renovation of the Scola Levantina, the place was restored in memory of the Holocaust.

In contrast to the Scola Kohanim, the *Yeshibhah Luzzatto*, the other "Scola" opened in the Ghetto Nuovo in the 16th century, can be well visualized although

While the *midhrashim* in the Ghetto Nuovo attest the survival and reawakening of a still potent religious spirit, an equal determination to recover is revealed by the extension of the Ghetto boundary with the opening in 1633 of the new sector called the *Ghetto Nuovissimo*, with its availability of more dwellings and a decided improvement in the actual conditions of residence. Contrary to what a consolidated historiographic tradition maintains, it was not a sharp increase in population or consequent requirements for more space that necessitated the new group of houses granted to the Jews alongside Rio della Macina (Rio di Ghetto Nuovo), but actually a shrewd response from the *Cinque Savi* to a request from the Levantines and Ponentines, in March 1633, begging them to set aside a small area containing houses more spacious and less modest than those in the current area of confinement, so that the added incentive of the availability of dignified homes would attract more Sephardic family groups to Venice, to inject new life into commercial activity after the hiatus caused by the plague. The *Cinque Savi* conducted a survey, and found at least 34 empty houses in the Ghetto Nuovo and Ghetto Vecchio, resulting not only from the heavy death toll caused by the plague, but also from the number of people who had emigrated to escape the contagion. Nevertheless, fully aware of the value of new blood and new features of attraction to the exhausted Venetian economy, they agreed to open a new sector that would act as a magnet to any merchants considering a move to the Lagoon. Their report to the Senate says, "Among these houses, 32, there are the houses of Ca' Zanelli, houses of considerable condition, size, and nobility ... ", drawing immediate attention to the sharp difference in quality between the new area and the other sectors of the Jewish quarter. However, they accompanied this favourable description with a constraint as to their precise use: the offer of a residential area sufficiently decent for 20 families of new immigrants was approved, provided that this brought immediate material advan-

98

tages to the State coffers, in other words, without in any way altering the letting system that had been operating for over a century, nor the traditional relations between landlords and tenants. In this way, because of its very purpose, the Ghetto Nuovissimo was, from the outset, always a separate sector, sharply distinct from the others by virtue of its clean streets, its noble palaces, and the social and economic level of its inhabitants. Besides this, it had a different

place in the overall city context, far from the functions performed by the other two Ghettos.

Venice - Ghetto Nuovo: houses on the Rio di Ghetto Nuovo, looking towards the Ghetto Nuovissimo

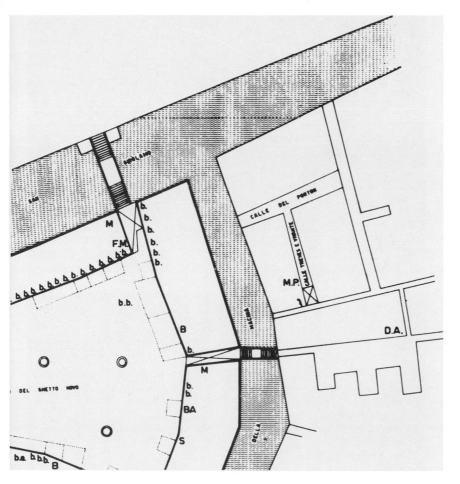

Map of the Ghetto Nuovissimo

Venice - Bridge and houses of the Ghetto Nuovis-➤
simo

The particular location of the Ghetto Nuovissimo, the motives that led to its institution, and its overall configuration, together lend it an urban character quite different from either of the other Ghettos. More than anything, in fact, it seems like an appendage to the Campo di Ghetto Nuovo, but totally devoid of the welter of activity and commercial vitality that typified the earlier sector; there were no pawn nor second-hand shops, such as had, in the course of one century, taken over every available space in the Campo (Carletto), nor is there any record of synagogues or *midhrashim* to show that there was a dedication to study and prayer, except for one *mezà*, or school for young children. Besides this, it was off the beaten track, so its isolation made it different in this respect from the Ghetto Vecchio.

It was primarily a residential quarter, with houses more spacious and welcoming than those of the adjacent sectors, sometimes real little palaces, fit to accommodate families of prestige and often vast wealth, enticed to Venice by the possibilities that such an attractive commercial centre still offered — which was exactly what the Sephardim who made the request wanted. (The *Treves* and *Vivante* palaces are the most tangible examples, both for their façades on the internal lanes and those that look over the Rio di San Girolamo and the Rio della Macina respectively, and for their interior schemes.) The sympathy of the *Cinque Savi* towards these aims may have been motivated by a nascent attitude that was to become steadily more blatant during the late 17th and early 18th centuries: with an about turn, sensational in its way, but not inconsistent with the Republic's traditional pragmatism when faced with an obviously difficult economic situation — above all in the credit sector, due to the *Università's* heavy indebtedness for the maintenance of the banks — Venice

99

The Ghetto Nuovissimo is the smallest of the three sectors, and also the least definite in its boundaries. For centuries, land registers and other documents show it as occupying, on its western and northern sides, the corner where the Rio della Macina meets the Rio di San Girolamo, connected by a wooden bridge to the portico that leads into the Campo di Ghetto Nuovo, and clearly shut off on its eastern side from the neighbouring Servi Convent. On the southern side, however, it can be seen that the original portico and gate have given way to a rather vague boundary situation, where an increasing number of houses along the Rio della Macina and the Calle della Macina have been

gradually taken in. It seems that only in the course of the 18th century did this spread towards the south occur, when it even took into the Ghetto area a "fire station" in Calle della Macina (now in the Ghetto Nuovissimo) intended to serve a wider residential area. On the other hand, the interior plan is quite simple. Three ample blocks of houses are separated by two intersecting lanes, the first terminating in an imposing portico at the southern end, the second distinguished at its eastern end from the present Calle degli Ormesini by a large gateway with a rusticated cornice.

must have decided to attract to the Rialto centre those very merchants whom, for so long, it had kept away from the city or segregated in the Ghetto, in order to substitute "separate" or "foreign" Jews for the class connected with moneylending. In short, in the eyes of today's scholars, the Ghetto Nuovissimo may additionally assume this precise historical significance.

It is probable that, as happened in the Ghetto Vecchio, the first row of houses in the Ghetto Nuovissimo too, crossed by the portico with the dividing gateway, was originally not actually included in the area of segregation. In this direction, however, the affinities with the Ponentine or Sephardic quarter, although to a minor extent, given the size of the new sector, can be seen largely from the placenames that seem to have been already established by the 18th century, going by contemporary land registers (Carletto). Here too, in fact, a street, the principal one, holding the most original palaces, some with noble entrances and façades vaguely reminiscent of Sansovino, takes its name from two of the richest families who lived there, Treves and Vivante, active in Venice mainly in the second half of the century of Enlightenment. The other is called the *Calle del Porton,* from the fact that it is closed at one end by the Ghetto's second gate (*portone*), erected to delimit the discrimination. These are marginal affinities, but they lead to a single conclusion which is the true basic reality: even a sector that may seem privileged and in many respects different from the others still remains a kind of "seraglio" scarred by the same marks of discrimination that have characterized every Italian ghetto.

100

Venice - Ghetto Nuovissimo: Calle del Porton

Title page of *Discorso circa il Stato de gl'Hebrei* by ▶
Simone Luzzatto, Calleoni, Venice 1638

DISCORSO
CIRCA IL STATO
DE GL'HEBREI.

Et in particolar dimoranti nell'inclita Città di
VENETIA,

DI SIMONE
LVZZATTO
Rabbino Hebreo,

*Et è vn appendice al Trattato dell' openioni e Dogmi de
gl' Hebrei dall'vniuerfal non diffonanti, e de
Riti loro più principali.*

IN VENETIA, M DC XXXVIII.

Appreffo Gioanne Calleoni.
Con Licenza de' Superiori.

The history of the Venetian Jews, as of all Jews in the Diaspora, alternates between periods of relative stability and phases of preoccupying threat. Just as the terrible event of the plague was followed by a hopeful attempt at recovery and the calmer situation in which the Ghetto Nuovissimo was set up (1633) and Ashkenazi conditions were improved (1634), these were followed in turn by a further grave and unexpected time of risk for the whole community during the Feast of Lots in 1636. "Purim 5396 (1636) turned from joy to sorrow for the whole community, and misfortunes began for the general public and for the individual" says Leon Modena in his *Autobiografia*. Two Jews, Grassin Scaramella and Sabbadin Catalano, reported by a fellow Jew, were discovered to have been involved in the theft of 70,000 ducats from the *Merceria*; other innocent Jews became implicated, and the Ghetto was closed and attacked "by nobles, citizens and common folk ... for, as is the custom, when someone sins the entire community pays for it". So great was the danger of even an immediate expulsion that the Doge appointed a sort of arbitration committee to investigate the entire event and settle the emergency situation. This successful intervention had an important secondary outcome.

The Jewish *Università* managed to come through, as had happened many times in the past, but this time they decided that they should express, through the mouth of one of their most illustrious spokesmen, a precise assertion of their own importance in Venetian society. No longer content with passive reaction, they contrived to convert the unjust accusation into a pretext for something positive.

Among the Jewish representatives chosen to be on the committee was Rabbi Simone Luzzatto (1583-1663), one of the most famous exponents of the moderate progressive wing of the Ghetto's body of rabbis. For him it was not simply a case of resolving a tricky situation, certainly no novelty in the history of the Diaspora; conscious of the danger incumbent upon the whole community, he felt that the best defence against the inevitable spread of hostile public opinion would be a realistic, once-for-all explanation of Judaism, concentrating particularly on claiming that the Jews played a necessary and irreplaceable role within the unstable economy of the nevertheless "illustrious city of Venice". So was conceived his *Discorso circa il Stato de gl'Hebrei*, one of the most important texts ever to come out of Venetian Jewish society. The celebrated work was printed by the Calleoni press in 1638 and, undoubtedly conditioned by such a genesis, presents itself as a most sharp and articulate counter argument against every possible prejudice or specific accusation. Luzzatto does this by means of a thoughtful and detailed analysis of Venice's economic status; while praising its quality and reputation, he also reveals the weaknesses that only the Jewish contribution can effectively deal with, being the most efficient and appropriate system evolved by any of the city's resident foreign groups. He goes back to the form of the Renaissance myth of Venice already used by other Jewish authors like Abrabanel and De Pomis, but avoids the presupposed metahistorics on which the interpretations of those writers was based, anchoring his argument, instead, to a realistic economic and political dimension. In line with the widespread view of his time, he praises the greatness and stability of the city's institutions and celebrates its wealth and magnificence, achieved mainly as a result of the profit it drew from mercantile exercise, but sharply points out that the withdrawal of Venetian merchants onto dry land would inevitably place *La Serenissima* on the downward path unless their place on the sea were filled by the "Hebrew nation". The volume of business the Jewish community had in fact procured through being able to utilize their superior relations with economic centres in the Levant, and the total input of around 220,000 ducats contributed to the State coffer in duties, rents and taxes, without requiring any expenditure for the maintenance and supervision of the Ghetto, made it an already integral part of the Republic. "That the

102

Hebrews contribute some considerable emolument to the illustrious City of Venice and that to this extent they may number themselves among the integrating portions of Her common people, I would esteem not to be such a daring and discordant suggestion as to offend the delicate feelings of still highly scrupulous souls," he declares with conviction, and it becomes clear that this assertion is the central theme of the Rabbi's argument, supported in the last "consideration" in his *Discorso* by a detailed picture of the Jewish condition in its many-sided expressions.

As many have commented, Luzzatto's words contained the most useful response, in that situation, to any possible attack on the Ghetto, expressed on lines in keeping with the Venetian State's characteristic pragmatism. But no one can ignore the fact that it must also be seen as an act of stout courage, alongside the almost contemporary *Historia* by Leon Modena, aiming, after so long, to publicize the authentic reality about a "nation" which Venice had already kept in a state of segregation for over a century, which had not been suffered in any comparable way by any other ethnic group living in the city.

By common consensus of historians, based also on abundant direct documentation, the span of time from the 1640s to the end of the 17th century marks the beginning of the downward slide in Ghetto affairs, in close connection, of course, with the political and economic crisis in the Venetian Republic. Venice was torn between the anti-Jewish attitude of a section of its conservative aristocracy, jealous of their commercial reputation in the Mediterranean, which they were now obliged to yield, in part, to the Sephardim, and the need, imposed by the commercial decline itself, to keep the Jewish resource active. In the years around the middle of the century, therefore, it tried to balance its policy between slight concessions to Ashkenazic and Sephardic requests and constant fiscal pressure on all the "nations". These tax burdens were borne by the Ghetto Vecchio merchants, but began to make more and more cracks in the already weakened Ghetto Nuovo banks. So in the 1660s, not finding among its own members sufficient capital to put aside for the maintenance of the credit market, the *Università* made a perhaps incautious decision and went outside the Ghetto to request credit. This action was followed by sometimes inadequate management, and by the early 18th century, with the accumulation of interest, the sums were to reach excessive figures. This was the real start of the community structure's breakdown. As the tension with the traditional Turkish enemy increased and the Mediterranean ports became less safe, signs of crisis became steadily more obvious at all levels, economic, social and spiritual. The State's ever harsher and more insistent demands for money from the Ghetto's apparently inexhaustible reserve prompted an early attempt among the "nations" to spread the burden more evenly, indirectly compromising the credit market. After that, inevitably, the progressive worsening of the situation set off a slow stream of migration from the Ghetto Vecchio towards Amsterdam or the Tyrrhenian ports, which offered greater promise of security and economic progress. This pro-

103

Venice - Correr Civic Museum: 17th C. Venetian flag (watercolour)

Venice - Museum of Jewish Art: ornament for the Scrolls of the Law (*rimmon*); late 17th C. Venetian art

duced an irreversibile decline with palpable psychological repercussions.

As can happen at times of sharpest depression, the unstable situation, while driving more sensitive souls towards a deeply pessimistic view of temporal and spiritual realities (which found perfect expression in the work of Mosheh Zacuto), also stimulated, by contrast, the spread of a desire for renewal among both cultured and common people. This seems for some years to have been satisfied by the success of the Shabbethan movement, which hailed Shabbethay Tzebhi as the Messiah sent to save Israel and Nathan of Gaza as his prophet (see p.105). But these were moments of brief enthusiasm, unable to wipe out a mounting feeling of doom. Deep disappointment at the failure of the false Messiah was followed by the outbreak, after years of tension, of yet another war between Venice and the Turk, and the eventual peace left the Venetian economy exhausted and the state of the Ghetto irremediably compromised. The Republic's repeated request for 150,000 ducats a year to finance the war effort, and the fiscal pressure, continuously rising despite attempted opposition by various "nations" combined with the increasing debt contracted to keep the banks alive, were once again the factors that led, in the 1690s, to a situation of acute anxiety which was to scar the Jewish quarter for ever. "The decline of the shop" records a resolution of the community's General Chapter in 1697, taken to "moderate the luxury and superfluous expense" flaunted by some families in disregard of the prevailing situation, "and the scarcity of profits in this market place, the high sums of debts to which our *Università* finds itself subject, and the supreme command of the very excellent Senate for the punctual payment of the many current taxes, and also the making good of past omissions, these having to be spread among a scarce number of contributors, there being unfortunately many families either declined or departed form the city, place on us the very heavy and almost insupportable burden."

Venice - The Ghetto on a perspective map published by Stefano Scolari in 1677

Besides the phenomenon of Sephardic emigration to safer ports, another characteristic aspect of the Venetian Jewish socio-economic story in the late 17th century was the constant tension between the imposition of "burdens" and levies by the State, and the continual resourceful but doomed attempts to evade them by the "nations" of the Ghetto, who were already in debt principally on account of the pawnbroking banks. Historians have calculated that in the hardest decade, the Veneto-Turkish war of 1681-91, the State absorbed, besides the standard contributions, at least 400,000 ducats of Jewish capital, causing, besides the inevitable though useless protests, continual friction between Ashkenazim and Sephardim about a fairer internal distribution of the taxes. In 1685, after far-reaching discussion, it was decided to replace the normal procedure for the election of tax collectors, which provided for the choice of "arbiters" whose decisions everyone had to abide by, with a system based on a fairer subdivision of the entire sum demanded between the individual "nations" each of which would then organize collections

from individual persons within it. Ten years later the Sephardim, once again, in their constant search for defensive strategies, fell back on the scheme of accepting even life-annuities to alleviate the increasing burden, besides deciding — as a Levantine document tells — to pawn some of the silverware from their only recently "refounded" synagogue. All these expedients could but temporarily stave off alarming situations of debt. The severe weight resting on the banks, who were now, furthermore, subjected to supervision by the *Quaranta al Criminal*, on top of the fiscal pressure requiring ever higher demands to be met, soon brought the Ghetto to a state of debt that proved, in fact, irreversible.

As had happened at other times of social or economic depression in Jewish history, this strong atmosphere of anxiety fostered the spread of acute pessimism about the human condition, combined with expectancy of the imminent coming of the Messiah and the redemption he was supposed to bring. In a climate saturated with Cabalistic ideas since the late 16th century, heavily stimulated by influences from Safed, the Venetian Rabbi Mosheh Zacuto, active between 1645 and 1673, with his noticeable inclination towards the Jewish mystical tradition, made himself spokesman of these controversial feelings, vitually preparing the ground for an event that was to perturb the Ghetto in the 1660s. In a discourse rich in messianic implications in his dramatic work *Yesodh 'olam* (The Foundation of the World) centred on the figure of Abraham, he confronts the problem of the path by which Man, with his idealistic dedication, can heal the rift in the cosmos between the human dimension and the divine. Then, in another literary tour de force, the *Tophteh 'arukh* (Hell Explained), decidedly influenced by echoes of Dante and even more by the theme of the disputation between the Devil and the dead man, he offers not only a gloomy and obsessive vision of the hereafter, but also such an agonizing and distressing image of human existence that it almost suggests, by contrast, a renewal occuring in the near future. So when, in 1666, news reached Venice that a new Messiah had emerged in Smyrna (Izmir) in the person of Shabbethay Tzebhi, and that his charm and reputation had already attracted vast ranks of followers, the Ghetto suffered an absolute trauma, both at the official level, in the positions taken by the rabbis, and at the common level.

Shabbethay proclaimed himself the Messiah, publicly celebrated his mystic marriage to the Torah, and went on to preach the ascetic life in order to bring nearer final redemption. He brought about transformations in the traditional liturgy and exhorted his audiences to penitence and asceticism. In Venice, in the enthusiasm created by his movement among a large section of the Ghetto's population in spite of some doubts and the silence imposed by the rabbis, festivities were abolished, rigid penitential schemes adopted, and there was a vast movement towards public repentance which at first did not displease even the most orthodox and conservative rabbi of the time, Shemu'el Aboaf. All the agitation and fervid expectancy, however, soon brought arguments and internal friction, closely followed by the deepest and bitterest disillusionment. When the news got about that the false Messiah had suddenly been converted to Islam, changing his name for the occasion to Mohamed Effendi, all enthusiasm crumbled. Nor could the confidence of his still incredulous followers be restored by the journey, in 1668, of Shabbethay's prophet, Nathan of Gaza, attempting to sustain the theory that false conversions were necessary by divine order, so as to permit the Messiah, after his ascent into Heaven, to accomplish his mission. Nathan was allowed into the Ghetto only on the intercession of a few Venetian nobles, and was then publicly repudiated by the rabbis, his ideas pronounced the fruit of a sick mind, all documents relating to the "myth" of Shabbethay destroyed, and the study of the *qabbalah* itself forbidden to minds insufficiently prepared. Thus the Shabbethan movement left not a trace behind, and the sad economic reality returned with all its worries and hardships.

Shabbethay Tzebhi in an engraving from *The Counterfeit Messiah* (18th. C)

The tendency towards mysticism in the air at that time, and the widespread fervour and enthusiasm in public opinion, managed to influence some of the more genuine expressions of the public spirit. The best known and most celebrated curtain for the Ark of the Covenant (*parokheth*) that the Venetian Jewish community still boasts today cannot perhaps be clearly understood in its symbols and its sophisticated design and composition unless it is seen in the light of those years, so deeply marked by messianic presences and Cabalistic stimuli. The valuable embroidery, a fine design in gold thread on blue silk, belongs to the Scola Levantina, where it is traditionally displayed for the feast of *Shabhu'oth* (Feast of Weeks). The embroideress's primary intention was obviously to represent the fundamental

106 event celebrated by the Feast of Pentecost, the gift of the *Torah* on Mount Sinay, and the "golden" city of Jerusalem. The design shows this in three parts. The top section depicts the gift of the Law on the cloud-wrapped mountain peak, according to *Exodus* XIX, 16: "*Wayhi bayyom hashshelishı ... — And it came to pass on the third day, when it was morning, that there were thunders and lightnings, and a thick cloud upon the mount, and the voice of a trumpet exceeding loud; and all the people that were in the camp trembled*" embroidered in full. In the middle section appear three peaks, Mount Sinay bears the tablets with the Ten Commandments, and another (Tziyon?) reminds one of *Psalm* LXVIII, 17: "*Lammah teratztzedhun harim gabhnunnim... — Why look ye askance, ye high mountains, at the mountain which God hath desired for his abode? Yea, the Lord will dwell in it for ever,*" while a river descends towards the sea, busy with shipping, after *Psalm* CIV, 25-26: "*Zeh hayyam gadhol urḥabh ... — Yonder is the sea, great and wide ... There go the ships*". Lastly, the lower part shows the walls of Jerusalem, rich with many verses from Isaiah. In the medallion below the gate of the Holy City appears the name of the embroideress — Stella, wife of Isacco Perugia, died in 1673 — together with the date indicating the beginning of

the work 5394 (1634) (D. Peer). She decided to embellish the central image further by including in the outer frame many other verses alluding to the Temple City and to Sinay, the most famous being certainly *Psalm* CXXXVII, 5: "*'Im'eshkaḥekh Jerushalayım tishkaḥ yemini — If I forget thee, O Jerusalem, let my right hand forget her cunning*". It is nevertheless evident from the choice of details and their arrangement in the figurative text that the entire picture could also allude to deeper meanings closely connected with the messianic and prophetic atmosphere of the mid-17th century, perhaps expressing one of the more common sentiments current in public opinion (Piattelli). It is most likely that the peaks shown are intended to refer to the mountains of sacred tradition, and to the values ascribed to them in ancient books. They are supposed to symbolize the moral strength which gives stability to

the true faith, together with the revelation of the word of God to the world and His onnipresence. All these themes achieve their synthesis in the Temple and in the city that is the symbol of the union between the people and the peace that redemption will bring to mortals, as if meaning the gathering of human strength at the intervention of the redeeming will of God through the Messiah. Stella, a simple believer from the Venetian Ghetto, has managed by her own skill and devotion to convey a message in these splendid images that seems to transcend the plain, literal illustration of the Bible, expressing instead an entire generation's yearning for renewal at a time of profound crisis, and handing it down in time.

Venice - Ghetto Nuovo, Museum of Jewish Art: 17th C. *parokheth*, the work of Stella Perugia

never accepted by orthodox opinion yet often performed, though doubtless with a pure heart and the intention only to protect against evil.

Nearly all the crucial moments of life were touched by it, but among the most curious practices must be mentioned that whereby people attempted, by means of amulets, to protect the lives of a new-born child and his mother from the forces and spirits of evil until the moment of *milah* (circumcision). "When a male child is born to a man, his friends make merry with him saying, be of good fortune, and some are in the habit of putting certain amulets in the four corners of the mother's room on which is written *Adam and Eve, go away Lilith*, and the name of three Angels; they say it is to protect the child from witches, but I rule that he who does not wish to do so shall stop putting them up, for not only is it not based on any precept, but moreover is vanity" records Leon Modena faithfully but objectively in his *Historia* (f.94). One of these "bulletins" or amulets, which has come down to us, indeed presents in the outer ring the formula mentioned by Modena against Lilith, the demon figure, probably of Sumerian origin, sometimes presented by Hebrew literature in the *Talmudh* and the *midhrash* as Adam's second wife, after his separation from Eve, and the mother of demons, or sometimes as his original wife, who dared to claim absolute equality with man, and then became an evil power against mothers and their new born babies; mystical tradition, furthermore, holds that she was the wife of Samael and mistress of evil. The inner ring, by contrast, has verse 7 from *Psalm* XCI as a protective device: "*Yippol mitztzidekha 'eleph urbhabhah miminikha 'eleykha lo' yiggash — A thousand shall fall at thy side and ten thousand at thy right hand, but it shall not come nigh thee*", while the equally defensive writing in the centre, *Shadday* (Omnipotent), is surmounted by the crown of the divine presence and accompanied below by the Star of David. Truly, sometimes the anxieties and worries of an age are brought home to us by small pieces of evidence of little apparent value.

It was to such creations that the development of ideas concerned with the mystic outlook led, and in an atmosphere pregnant with facile suggestions it also fostered the proliferation of popular beliefs, not to say superstitions, that had been present in Hebrew culture for centuries. In the late 17th century, the most palpable sign of this was perhaps the renewed spread of practices connected with the "magic" aspect of the *qabbalah*, a sort of "white magic"

Emblems of some Jewish families in Venice

In Venice, as in other communities of the Diaspora, it was common practice for prominent Jewish families to adopt their own armorial bearings to distinguish them from other families or simply to record ancient lineages. A whole range of quite varied devices chosen to perpetuate a name may be seen on prayer book bindings, usually made of silver, which were a traditional wedding gift, in *Kethubboth* (marriage contracts), in certain manuscripts and, more than anywhere, on the tombstones in the San Nicolò cemetery. The origin of such emblems generally has absolutely no connection with the feudal and court tradition of heraldry, which is clearly demonstrated by their distinguishing features and the frequently observable fact that different branches of the same family have adopted sometimes quite substantially altered versions of the same device. Whereas the "Golden Book of Italian Nobility" registers families who obtained their titles from the King of Italy or the Emperor of Austria, the most prominent Jewish family groups — with the exception of a few *marrani* who decided to keep the insignia of their Spanish baptismal godfathers, a few exceptional Jews who had risen to noble dignity in spite of the state of inferiority imposed by law and, obviously, others who had been elevated during the period of emancipation — wishing to imitate the non-Jewish nobility, had since the humanistic era assumed either symbolic emblems referring to their role within Jewish society, such as the blessing hands for the *Kohen* (priests) and the jug and basin for the washing of hands for the Levites, or devices alluding either to their own Jewish name or to their town of origin, such as the ladder for the Sullam family or the cock for the Luzzatto family, or simply emblems handed down by tradition, referring to moral virtues or distinctive qualities — in short, a vast range of devices that many Ghetto families in Venice decided to adopt for themselves.

108

Venice - Museum of Jewish Art: Precious 18th C. prayerbook binding, a wedding gift, with the arms of the Trieste family (right) and the Vivante family (left)

LEVI

On the quartered shield, the emblem of the Levites is accompanied by the psalm, which indicates justice (*Psalm* XCII, 13), the pyramid (constancy), and a ship (the Zebhulun tribe on the sea)

MODENA

The emblem of Leon Modena shows a leopard holding in its paws the *lulabh*, or palm leaf, used for the feast of the Tabernacles (*Sukkoth*)

LEVI DEL BANCO

One of the oldest Ghetto families. The five roses perhaps indicate gentleness in the courtly sense, as the combination of all the virtues

DE POMIS

The emblem of the famous doctor's family shows an apple tree (*pomo*) supported by two lions (strength) and surmounted by a comet. At the base is a rose (gentleness?)

SULLAM

The emblem of the Sullam family (ladder in Hebrew) shows a five-step ladder (the *Torah* which leads upwards) supported by two lions and surmounted by a crown, symbol of the divine presence

LUZZATTO

The Luzzatto emblem either derives from those of their city of origin (Lausitz) or has a symbolic meaning: freewill (cock), if under the guidance of the Torah (stars and moon), produces good works (ear of corn)

CURIEL

The flaming heart pierced by two arrows on the emblem of this ancient Sephardic family indicates love combined with skill

UZIEL

In Hebrew, Uziel means "the Lord is my strength". Their emblem includes devices clearly associated with the name's semantic value

FOÀ

The emblem of the great printing family Foà bears the palmtree (justice) with the Star of David among its fronds, supported by two lions

CAMERINO

The lion bearing an upward pointing arrow (strength and skill), surmounted by sunbeams dexter, forms the Camerino emblem, a family of Italian Jews, in Venice from the 18th century

GENTILI

The heart, indicating mental and physical balance, surmounted by three stars perhaps alluding to divine law, is the emblem of the Gentili family, living in Veneto mainly in the 18th century

109

ERRERA

The emblem of the Sephardic family Errera, thriving in Venice from the 18th century, bears two fishes facing dexter and sinister linked by an S-shaped line

FINZI

The emblem of the Veneto branch of the Finzi family shows a hand with the index finger pointing up to a crescent moon, meaning that the Torah leads to heaven (a silver hand with pointing index finger is used when reading the scriptures)

VIVANTE

The Vivante family, Sephardim from Corfu, living in Venice from the mid-18th century, have on their emblem a hand grasping a banner (faith?)

GUETTA

The Sephardic Guetta family, in Venice from the early 19th century, has a shield divided per fesse; above, a classic portal, probably referring to the Jerusalem Temple; below, the fesse, the mark of a gentleman

FRANCHETTI

The Franchetti family were thriving during the age of emancipation; their emblem shows the lion of strength and justice on a red field, alluding to life's struggles

TREVES DE BONFILI

Barons of the Napoleonic era, the Treves de Bonfil(i) family has a quartered shield; the dove with the olive branch implies peace, while the tree and stars, the ship, and the wheatsheaf are all Biblical symbols

In the crisis that was undermining the Republic, the Ghetto's last century of life was, as it were, punctuated by the social and economic phases that led inexorably to the community's fall. The relationship between the State and the *Università* had been stable for some time, but in the last thirty years things became more tense and difficult. Venice had an insatiable need for money, being again involved in Mediterranean skirmishes early in the century, and the Jews found it impossible to pay off the debt already contracted. This, combined with an incredible accentuation of the so-called "lending policy" which raised the Ghetto's debt to a figure that could never be met, brought about the introduction of an unprecedented scheme that, without yielding any positive results, conditioned the Jews' entire remaining period of cohabitation with *La Serenissima*. On the one hand, the State evolved a tangle of strategies in the search for new ideas to save the situation, while on the other, the Jews put forward an endless stream of involved plans that did nothing but create new debts to pay off old ones and, in trying to redeem a society already weakened at its foundations, succeeded only in hastening its unhappy demise.

From the many fact-finding enquiries ordered by the Senate, the only constant element that emerged was "disorder"; this not only applied to the difficult running of the banks (which effectively fell on the entire *Università*), where the proposal for stricter control by the appointed authorities produced no satisfactory result, but more radically concerned the question of the apportioning of taxes and levies for the payment of the enormous debts. This created continual friction between the "nations" and bad feeling against individuals who declared themselves "foreigners" or "in transit" to evade the immense burden, provoking an incessant search for better ways of spreading the load, but all to no avail. In 1722, confronted with the repeated attempts by Jewish families to leave the Ghetto for safer ports, and realizing that the community's total debt had reached an exhorbitant level, the *Cinque Savi* proposed, as an emer-

110

Venice - Museum of Jewish Art: 18th C. silver ewer for the washing of hands of the *Kohanim* (priests)

Prayer book for the day of *Kippur* (Atonement) in Sephardic ritual. Bragadina Press, Venice 1792

to suspend all debt for six months and then start again on the basis of calculations and a procedure acceptable to all. So on 4 September 1736, after the Venetian nobles had accepted the proposal, the three "nations" of the Ghetto also finally arrived at an agreement, signed by the *Università's* official scribe, Samuel Levi Muya, governing their internal matters, "to accommodate," runs the text, "and assuage any difference that may arise among the nations ... after the execution of the Termination carried out by the *Inquisitorato Eccellente sopra l'Università* itself during the day 10 July 1736". Although this was not the solution to every problem, it was indeed a start, later endorsed by the 1738 *condotta*, towards a less worrying situation for the Jewish economy, now sustained by fresh credit found in Holland and England. At the same time it was sunset for the old ruling class, leaving room for new families of "foreigners" whose conspicuous wealth was protected by State agreement to precise limits on annual taxation. It was not, however, a case of standardization nor, at first, of a complete change of tone after the volte-face of the fifties, not even for the new arrivals.

The belated opening to Jews of commercial opportunities in fields until then forbidden was followed, although the situation was still grave, by an inopportune protectionist squeeze put into effect by a vast section of the Venetian aristocracy with the intention of imposing precise restrictions on the Ghetto merchants, particularly in the olive oil market, which was concentrated largely in their hands, through Corfu. This created friction within the Venetian ruling class itself, between the liberal tendency of a minority who were aware of the still considerable Jewish contribution, and the pressure from a broad group of nobles, headed by Andrea Tron, with anti-Jewish leanings, and it was the latter who first prevailed in the seventies, even inspiring, in 1777, perhaps the most unfavourable and severe *condotta* issued in the last two centuries of Ghetto life. The first part, consisting of 96 paragraphs, contained a long series of strict impositions on the

suggested turning once again to loans and arrangements with creditors. This, however, was doomed to failure. In 1732 the Senate, ever desperate for the Jewish contribution, attempted, with a decree, to attract fresh groups of Sephardic Jews from Leghorn for the express purpose of reviving the exhausted trade. In 1735 the new authority, faced with inevitable disaster (historians speak of insolvency and bankruptcy), found itself obliged to air the suggestion of an expulsion from the Ghetto. This alarmed the Venetians possibly more than the Jews themselves and had the effect of a common enemy, at last forcing creditors and debtors into agreement. They decided

gency measure, to unify the three "nations" for administrative purposes, and to delegate all control over the Ghetto to a single authority, the *Inquisitorato sopra l'Università degli Ebrei*. But its attempt to save the Ghetto, whose ruin would damage the entire Venetian economy, ran straight into such a tangled and insoluble situation that the Jewish ruling class, with an ever dwindling number of rich families to count on,

pawnbroker banks, and later regulations included a range of harsh restrictions in the commercial sector, dictated by a decidedly rigid conservative outlook. Community affairs had sunk to an all-time low, a situation which had immediate repercussions on an already exhausted economy, and could not fail to induce the Venetian authorities to intervene once again, in a characteristic way, to put matters right.

The atmosphere of more relaxed coexistence that prevailed during the last twenty years of the century was created by a conference called barely two years later, in 1779, and recalled in 1786, that was supposed to lay down the premises for the 1788 *condotta*, in which, under the stimulus of the new enlightened "approachability" the Senate tried to mitigate the more limiting restrictions in force, to some extent modifying a condition of real anxiety. But the State's thoughtful initiatives in many commercial fields were in fact of concrete advantage only to a small number of Ghetto merchants, and in this way, against the background of the community's progressive decline as an administrative structure, favoured the establishment of a group of families who then became able to invest their

capital profitably (Luzzatto). This phenomenon is now accepted by recent historians. The more solid Jewish groups, in fact, found themselves advantaged by the new regulations in a number of ways: not only in the sphere of maritime trade, always a Jewish preserve, but also in the shipbuilding sector, with the concession — not new, however — of monopoly licences for the ownership of merchant ships, also in the development of the cereal trade, to which the Jews were admitted only after much hesitation but finally became recognized among the State food-supply contractors, and in openings in the industrial field, especially manufacturing, which, thanks to modern organization, was capable of high quality products. Thus, at the end of the century, with the Republic on the brink of ruin, the most obvious result of the lengthy series of State measures was actually the accentuation of fresh social differences within the *Università*, replacing the old squabbles between Germans and Sephardim. Although a small group of families were destined in the coming century to assume a prestigious role in Venetian society, a great number continued to lead insecure lives, clinging as a last hope to religious

traditions and Bible study.

In such a situation, the removal of the Ghetto gates and the brief experiment of democratic government in 1797, which gave Jews equality with other citizens, were certainly unexpected and sudden events after centuries of segregation, but the ensuing scenes of enthusiastic jubilation were accompanied by a sense of surprise and bewilderment, considering the gravity of the social problems. Indeed there had been no reforms or discussions that might have paved the way for such an event, nor could a certain enlightened openmindedness really have been expected to herald such a radical transformation. Many people believed the proclaimed values of equality and fraternity and managed to delude themselves that they were seeing the end of centuries-old segregation and standing before the "tree of liberty". The caution of a few, however, proved more realistic than the hopes of the many. The Ghetto gates were never re-erected, it is true, and centuries of discrimination had come to an end, but for the majority of the Jewish population, living in straitened circumstances, the "Ghetto" with all its pejorative implications was destined to survive for a long time yet.

112

Venice - Museum of Jewish Art: 18th C. Venetian Jews, from a picture illustrating the circumcision ceremony (*milah*) with greetings messages

Late 18th C. map of the Venetian Ghetto (private collection)

the three banks, open all day, situated at strategic points of the Campo, on fixed sites but with a "receipt" that could vary according to the choice of the operators, green, red or black. The continual flow of people towards the small second-hand trade or the credit market — from which Jews were excluded as customers — had effectively changed the district into an "open sector" the three entrance gates keeping the inmates in constant lively contact with surrounding society, for whom *far moscón* (the Hebrew *mashkon* means pledge or pawn) had become the common expression for pawning something, and the deprecatory corruption *Menacài* of the highly common *Mordekhay* denoted the prototype Jew, intent all day on "keeping shop" (Muazzo). The life led there, which in the heavily centralized structure of the urban layout involved the entire resident population, had no more than generic traits in common with the adjacent Ghetto Vecchio, with the exception of their religion, marked by the common liturgical rhythm of study and prayer. The constant movement in and out of the Ghetto Nuovo and the consequent variety of exchanges were in sharp contrast to the manner of operations in the Sephardic quarter, inhabited mainly by merchants occupied in international commerce, where the existing shops were geared to the inside, although they did not exclude outside customers. These shops, ranged along the Strada Maestra, were not involved in the second-hand trade nor in moneylending, but were closely concerned with the daily life of the two "nations" selling fruit and vegetables, meat and confectionery. Nearby was the bookshop in the Campiello delle Scuole, the Wayfarers' Inn with its twenty-four rooms, the Scola Levantina, the hospital in Calle dei Barucchi, and the newly fashionable coffee house on the right, a few steps from the Cannaregio portico. In short, two sharply distinct units still existed in the 18th century. The authorities tried to unite them in certain respects, but keep them clearly apart in others. Consequently the crisis affected each of them in a profoundly different way.

113

Historians involved in tracing the framework of the last century of the Ghetto's life have concentrated on the social and economic aspect, and this has sometimes led them to neglect the minor details of daily life, which are no less revealing than the "official" story. Yet it is easy to notice that the local image of the *hasèr* (meaning ghetto in Venetian-Jewish parlance), seen as a small world of minor events and daily facts and figures rooted in memory and popular tradition, dates back largely to the 18th century. It is from an analysis of land registers of that time that the Ghetto Nuovo reveals its true appearance, definitively transformed into a veritable commercial magnet, with about sixty rag-and-bone shops set up on the ground floors of very tall houses divided into ever-tinier apartments, and

When the new mentality of enlightenment spread in Venice, producing a feeling of newness and unfamiliar open-mindedness within established patterns, it was a rather tardy phenomenon which only in the later years of the 18th century produced in the ruling class a gentler attitude towards Jewish society. The old restrictions continued for most of the century, however, culminating in the squeeze of 1777, and had the power to affect not only commercial drive but also, most importantly, the rapport between Jews and Christians in the matter of "public morality".

The *Cattaver* officials had been at pains in the 17th and 18th century to keep Germans entirely separate from Levantines and Ponentines, so that the former would not, "for lack of dwellings" in the Ghetto Nuovo, go to join the residents in the Ghetto Vecchio. For very different reasons, and with far more justification, they insisted on a separation between adherents to different faiths. So Christians of all ages who had entered the houses of "Judeans" were reported, above all those under the age of sixteen, in the belief that any contact at this level was potentially dangerous. They were supported by the officials of the *Cinque Savi* when, in 1720, they forbade non-Jews in the sector they controlled to drink Kasher wine prepared to specific standards especially for Jews, and when, on various occasions, they intervened with some severity to stop Jews and Christians mixing during Carnival, although it was held to be a time of licence and lawbreaking. No less strongly indicative of the persistent determination to discriminate are the interventions of the *Esecutori contro la Bestemmia*, who hung a proclamation on the Ghetto gates reminding Christian women that it was strictly forbidden to stay overnight or do any work in a Jewish house, fully aware of the many legal and religious stumbling blocks that could be created (and still can) by the inevitable and not infrequent friendships between young Jews and young Christians. Most significant, a tablet set into a wall in the Ghetto Vecchio a few paces from the gateway leading to Cannaregio proclaims a drastic prohibi-

tion they made on 20 September 1704, as if to endorse the evidence of an intolerance typical of an age and record it for all time. "*His Serene Highness and the Gentlemen Esecutori contro la Bestemmia forbid any Jewish man or woman having been made Christian to visit or work under any pretext whatsoever in the Ghettos of this city*" reads the now barely legible inscription, and goes on to list, in case of transgression, "*rope, prison, galley, whip, pillory ...*" finally inviting would-be informers to report transgressors and offering lavish rewards to those that would lend themselves to such a deed. It was by way of a reminder, placed before the eyes of anyone who had just come in or was about to leave the quarter.

Venice - Correr Civic Museum: G. Grevembroch, *Gli abiti de' veneziani* p.50: *Jewish finesse*, the reception in the Ghetto of the Capitano Grande (Chief of Police)

Venice - Ghetto Vecchio: Stone tablet of 1704

Besides these discriminations, and in addition to heavy taxation, special contributions continued to be demanded from the Ghetto. These did indeed guarantee a tranquil life in the city but at the same time further endorsed the condition of humiliating inferiority under which the Republic held the Jews. Although it was not unreasonable that the expense of the guards at the gates and the night watchmen on the canals should have fallen on the Ghetto, not to mention the responsibility for keeping the water in them clean, it is also true that on top of the constant war levies, often running into high figures, there were sometimes extraordinary requests to meet reception expenses for some visiting authority who might have come to attend the military exercises on the Lido or a special feast in the Doge's Palace. The decorations and the banquets were all prepared with Jewish ducats, and it was often these that contributed even to the running of the nearby church of San Geremia. In exchange, it must be acknowledged that the authorities, through the guardians of public order, defended the Ghetto against assaults and intrusions from the populace, although such occurrences were rare in Venice compared with other places. Even in this case it was often Jewish financial intervention that served to ensure order and vigilance. The chief of police, called the *Messere* or *Capitano grande*, customarily went round the districts of the city as soon as he was appointed, to introduce himself to the people it would be his duty to oversee and protect. When he reached the Ghetto he was greeted with honours in the central square where a special seat had been set, and there, relates an 18th century source, "promising precise vigilance, whence they ever enjoy quiet sojourn ... he profited by a gratuity of sixty ducats, which was presented in the name of the *Università* by one of the Heads of the same". With malicious irony, the manuscript heads the page on which Grevembroch has illustrated the scene, "Jewish finesse" but the "finesse" was, as always, cunningly sought and absolutely obligatory.

115

In the course of the 18th century, the distrustful attitude towards the Jews found more restrained expression in Venice than in other parts of Italy, although no less significant. Elsewhere, the widespread anti-Jewish spirit pervaded the works of Medici or Ferretti, for instance, always hitting out at the "perfid Hebrew" on the plane of theological dispute, and those of Sessa and D'Arco, structured around social and economic themes and arguing the injurious weight of the Ghetto on the state economy, but it was neither credited nor accepted in the Republic. On the contrary, references to Jews to be found in Venetian documents or literary texts indicate a concern for Ghetto life that may well be linked to traditional preconceptions or stereotyped images but they never express the violent hatred or repulsion explicit elsewhere in conservative attitudes. Alongside the vast tracts accorded to the Jewish world in the works of the great historians of the Republic, from Sandi to Gallicciolli, references to Jews in more popular texts all seem to follow this tendency. The collection of Venetian proverbs and sayings produced in 1768-71 by the nobleman Francesco Muazzo (*Raccolta*) alternates, for example, between objective recording of the usages and customs of the Ghetto, albeit accompanied by a transcription of the famous anti-Jewish song *La Gnora Luna*, and a reserved admiration for certain illustrious Jews worthy of respect and esteem no less than other persons. A musical intermezzo, *La Conciateste* of 1735 harks back, without spiteful connotations, to the stereotype Jew utterly and expertly intent on usury; an intermezzo by Goldoni himself, *La Pelarina* of 1730 does not seem outrageous, but allows itself a good-humoured smile when he makes his character Volpiciona say: "*I am a Jew, not a poor man/ I am expert at pawnbroking,/ But honoured gentleman,/ Ask all the ghetto,/ I do not know the art of swindling*". The most immediate counterpart to this attitude at the popular level is to be found in moments of fun and shameless licence like the Carnival. When the Venetian people, never violently averse

116

to the Ghetto inhabitants, went out along the streets in fancy dress, they even dressed up, among their many disguises, as Jewish men and women; but what could have been their opportunity to give vent to their hostility in an unkindly deformed image stopped short, instead, at strong caricature, emphasizing already stereotyped physical features, carrying an account book instead of a prayer book, wearing the Jewish frock-coat, the *ṭalleyth*, in a deliberate mixture of sacred and profane, but never overstepping the bounds

of good-humoured irony. In popular "wisdom" consigned as always to sayings, the Jews do not appear as people to be shunned any more than other elements in a heterogeneous society. "From priests, friars, nuns, Jewish nuisances and Burano pests, Good Lord deliver us" runs the famous prayer, and the Jews do not even head the list!

Venice - Correr Civic Museum: "Jewish" carnival masks

It was probably the nobility and the authorities who felt most reserve towards the Jews. It is true that over the centuries many Venetian nobles did in fact take a genuine interest in Jewish culture; it is known that many intellectuals attended sermons by famous rabbis in the Ghetto, and many availed themselves of treatment from distinguished doctors; in another sphere, many enjoyed theatrical performances by Jewish actors on the occasion of *Purim*, the Feast of Lots. But it is also true that the aristocracy were initially so hostile to the Jews that they brought about the confinement of the "Judeans" as they were called, in the Ghetto, and later bitterly jealous of the commercial reputation they won, particularly in mercantile trade. In the 18th century, in the face of the disastrous situation of the Ghetto economy and the decline in international commerce, this tendency was reinforced at various levels, finding ideological support in the ultra-conservative view of Andrea Tron, incapable of allowing even the minutest Jewish expansion, which would not have been opposed by contemporary liberal creeds. The prime consequence of their attitude was the revival of traditional prejudices about Jewish wickedness and perfidy. These were no different from those held by the common people, but when expressed in socio-economic essays or in governmental decisions they became a more dangerous threat.

The most obvious indication of this is probably that Jews were obliged to take a special oath before a public notary, following a particular formula. A manuscript in the Correr Museum shows the scene of oath-taking with a Jew actually on his knees before the Doge and reads: "Whereas the Jews through their own fault have fallen from Grace, and for their own perfidy are become as servants and slaves of all the People, and much more of the Faithful, grown up in misery and iniquity, are regarded by all nations whatsoever in the shape of liars and unworthy; therefore to constrain them in some way not to be mendacious, they are obliged by the Prince and by the Magistrature to lend faith by touching the pen, this signifying the same as laying the hand on the Scriptures, written with a similar instrument". This unusual gesture, meaningless in itself, was used in its symbolic significance to accompany the corresponding formula, likewise reported: "*Et juravit tacto calamo more Hebreorum — And swore, having touched the pen in the Hebrew custom*" followed by Hebrew words probably similar to those lying in full view at the Doge's feet, alluding to the solemn oath in the name of God and undertaking not to fall short of the word given. This did not apply to other foreign groups in the city, at least not in such a humiliating form, and the fact that it was compulsory for Jews indicates once again the existence of a discriminatory separation that became gradually more overwhelming as time went on.

Venice - Correr Civic Museum: G. Grevembroch, *Gli abiti de' veneziani* p.3: *Jewish oath*

The most concrete expression of the anti-Jewish attitude was without doubt the *condotta* of 1777, by common consensus of most recent historians "a step backwards compared with preceding *condotte*" as Luzzatto called it, if not actually, in Bachi's words, "the most unfavourable that has ever been recorded in the entire history of the Venetian Diaspora". Anticipated by the latest of many refusals to grant subject status to Jews and conditioned by the nature of the 1775 anti-Jewish edict of Pope Pius VI Braschi, it was the product of the prevailing conservative anti-Semitic attitude, represented by Tron and largely supported by the *Cattaveri*, over the minority of more sensitive Senators prepared to be more accommodating towards the Ghetto. From the first, the conference called to revise existing re-

118 lations and decide the new regulations was unusually brisk in its deliberations and, opposed in vain by the pro-Jewish minority, drew up a "contract" which the Senate approved with a clear majority on 27 September 1777. Throughout its 96 paragraphs, phrased as if in hostile reply to a previous petition from the community, all aspects of Jewish life, civil and religious, were reviewed and regulated in a heavily restrictive plan. Many paragraphs touched on the vast problems of the mercantile sector and other activities that the Jews, especially the Sephardim, were trying to move into, while the former prohibitions in the commercial sector were added to by further, harsher ones attempting to block all Jewish initiatives in the agricultural sector. Renewed refusal of subject status was accompanied by the imposition of further levies on loans and banks. The intransigent paragraphs even included provisions that particularly harmed the interests of those social sectors of the Ghetto, mainly the Sephardim, towards which Venetian politicians had previously, even in that century, shown themselves well disposed. Order was given to liquidate certain Jewish-run factories and works unless they were authorized by special permits, the marketing of grain and the processing of merchandise, imported or not, was forbidden, and finally certain

limitations were imposed on the freedom of navigation, which could only disadvantage the "separate" Jews of the Levantine and Sephardic nations and in some cases give them a strong incentive to abandon the city for better destinations, to the serious detriment of the whole Ghetto. It is true that the rest of the *condotta*, as has been observed, did not touch the delicate problem of shipping licences held by Jews, nor greatly threaten the economic standing of certain leading families, but the combined effect of the prohibitions was inevitably such as to create, even in the eyes of the authorities themselves, an open state of tension so worrying that an immediate revision was clearly required to avoid its more damaging ef-

fects. Indeed, the conference called for this purpose in 1779 attempted to reverse much of the difficult situation, correcting perhaps ill-calculated or inopportune provisions, but it was another case of too little too late. The fate of the Jewish quarter, with that of the Republic itself, was already sealed.

Venice - The 1777 "*ricondotta*"

C A P I T O L I

DELLA RICONDOTTA

D E G L I   E B R E I

DI QUESTA CITTA', E DELLO STATO,

Estesi in esecuzione a' Decreti

DELL' ECCELLENTISS. SENATO

DE DI' 22. FEBBRARO 1776. E 23. AGOSTO 1777

ED APPROVATI

COL SOVRANO DECRETO

De dì 27. Settembre 1777.

M D C C L X X V I I.

PER LI FIGLIUOLI DEL QU. Z. ANTONIO PINELLI
STAMPATORI DUCALI.

Bahyà ibn Paquda, *Ḥobhoth hallebhabhoth* (The Duties of the Heart), translation into Ladino, Bragadina Press, Venice 1713

The only response that the Jewish community, for its part, was able to make to the worsening social and economic situation, besides exclusively commercial initiatives or expedients, was once again retrenchment into its own religious traditions and inherited faith. But this time it was different from previous centuries, manifested more at the level of popular awareness and emotional participation than high-minded intellectual contributions, the Ghetto's culture being by now incapable of expressing the high values of men like Elia Levita, Leon Modena and Simone Luzzatto. Although the phenomenon was not showy and conspicuous, as it would be in centuries to come, it is perceptible through different symptoms and manifold events. Whereas in the past the courage, sometimes of an entire "nation" had led to the building of the various synagogues and places of culture and study, often in open defiance of State bans, now, by contrast, there was a tendency for various sincere individuals, driven by genuine religious sentiment, to undertake the restoration and embellishment of certain places of worship, despite the difficult economic situation. This was the century, in fact, of the renovation of the *Scola Grande Tedesca* (1733), the completion of the decorations and the gilding of the *Scola Canton* (1736 and 1780), the great restoration of the *Scola Italiana* (1739), the opening of the *midhrash* in the *Scola Spagnola* (1733-6) and the ornamental alterations in the *Scola Levantina* (1782-6). However, those aesthetically enriched and more flamboyantly designed halls no longer heard the sermons of great rabbis, no longer listened to the intellectual debates of scholars of international reputation on matters of ritual; the rabbis of the 18th century still produced famous names like Isacco Pacifici, Giacobbe Saraval and Simone Calimani, but they could no longer contend with other centres of the Diaspora for a reputation that had formerly made Venice renowned throughout Europe. Even their few representatives of quality were obliged to support a congregation of worshippers who were still deeply bound by religious values, but no longer endowed with that elevated knowledge of Hebrew culture and language that had always distinguished the majority of Ghetto inhabitants. Sermons in Italian had by now become usual, and another phenomenon, seen sporadically in the 17th century, was increasing, concerning liturgical texts. It became necessary to translate the most important Hebrew works on morality (Rabbis Calimani and Saraval made the first translation of the *Pirkey 'abhoth — The Maxims of the Fathers*) and of devotion (the Bragadina press, sharing the Hebrew publishing sector with the Vendramina, published, for example, a fine Ladino edition of Bahyà ibn Paquda's well-known *Hobhoth hallebhabhoth — The Duties of the Heart,* for Sephardic use) — effectively supplanting the production of original texts or comments which had at one time taken the Venetian press to unsurpassed heights. In the same way it also became necessary to write educational texts in Italian (Calimani, again, published a Hebrew grammar), Hebrew being still read but not completely understood by most people. The more flexible contacts established between the Ghetto population and those outside — at the popular level, certainly not among the élite — were beginning to have a disruptive effect which detracted from people's feelings about their own tradition; the emotional content was still the same, but there was less cultural depth.

It is without doubt language, as always mirror of its users' social and cultural conditions, that best seems to reveal the nature of this tie with tradition, tenaciously persistent but certainly more superficial than in the past. Gradual detachment from the sacred tongue, mastered now by few and used only in services, was accompanied by the development, on all social levels, of that particular phenomenon typical in similar forms of all Italian ghettos, the Venetian-Jewish vernacular. It certainly expressed a constant awareness of liturgy and ritual, although the strong ingredient of Hebrewisms introduced into its distinctive texture of Venetian

Haggadhah shel Pesaḥ p.1, in Hebrew, with instructions in Italian written in Hebrew characters, and an introduction to the ritual in Venetian-Jewish vernacular, Vendramina Press, Venice 1740

The *Sedher* (Passover supper), from p.6 of a *Haggadhah* (narration) printed by the Vendramina Press, Venice 1740

dialect reflected a genuine emotional and sentimental rapport with the past rather than the living consciousness of a religious present. It originated when the Jews were first confined in the Ghetto. The Venetian dialect was assumed, without any marked deviations, in all its phonetic and syntactic peculiarities, and to it were added Hebrew or remembered but italianized German or Spanish words, not with any clannish and defensive intent in the face of the outside world, but rather to fill semantic areas that the dialect was unable to cover. In the present state of research, it appears to correspond neither to monogenetic theories about its origin propounded by scholars who believe all Jewish-Italian vernaculars to have derived, through a process of slow transformation, from a single, common, ancient, southern-central matrix, in the wake of Jewish groups migrating to various settlements in northern Italy, nor to the so-called polygenetic or archaistic hypothesis, which suggests instead that the languages used by Jews in the ghettos result from the survival of archaic forms of various local dialects that have been preserved in Jewish parlance by virtue of their segregation. Almost alone among Italian-Jewish vernaculars, the parlance of Venetian Jews continued to develop over centuries, as is documented by testimonies from both Jews and non-Jews, as the best means of expressing, with its subtle sarcasms and its tongue-in-cheek

allusions, the typical daily "world" of the Jewish quarter. By reason of its very nature, though, it remained a purely oral instrument, leaving Hebrew or Italian for written texts. Only after the 18th century — and this is rather significant — does evidence begin to appear of its additional use in written form, although strictly limited to important moments in religious life. It is not only on the occasion of *Purim*, the time of fancy dress and Carnival licence for everybody, including Jews, that a caprice in theatrical form, such as *La Mascheretta Veneziana* (L. Rialto, Venice, 1720), has recourse to the "language of the Hebrews", as Muazzo defined it, to utter in verse the invitation to celebrate the party: "*Amisi cari, mi v'invito de core / al seder de Purim, con tutt'amore / ... Sadisfevve / comodevve / alla cariega / che ve prega / la siora Chanà / la mia iscià / che tanto chen l'ha / in dir la parasah*" (Dear friends, I invite you from the heart to the Purim supper, with all my love ... Satisfy yourselves, make yourselves comfortable on the chair, as you are bidden by Mistress Chanà, my wife who has such grace in saying the Bible portion). The need to make the believing public understand the original sense of the story and the liturgical significance of the feast of *Pesaḥ* (Passover), with the precise instructions for the rules to be followed when preparing the same, made it necessary not only to republish the text of the *Haggadhah* (narration that is read at the *sedher* —

Passover supper) accompanied by a translation and explanation in Italian, although written in Hebrew characters (devised by Leon Modena), but also to have recourse to the parlance, also written in Hebrew characters, to describe the practice for preparing the celebration: "*La bona dona che va tuttavia caseriando la sua masaria ... Quest'altra qui fa pesaḥ ala casa e niente de hamez dentro ze lasa*" (The good woman who goes nevertheless making her household fit ... The other woman who prepares the home for *pesaḥ* (Passover) leaving nothing ḥamez (impure) within it). In short, a symptom of the sure survival of traditional values, constant adherence to the faith of their fathers, but also a detachment from the usual customs that can only be explained by incipient cultural decadence.

121

The authorities and the rabbis were conscious of this situation and at the same time aware of the dangers from the inexorable, slow infiltration of the first influences of Enlightenment. They were also anxious to confront a reality that was proving disquieting on the ideological and religious level because of another outburst in the 1730s of Cabalistic ideas, albeit in the prestigious name of Mosheh H. Luzzatto from Padua, and attempted to oppose all disruptive factors by acting in the only way then practicable — concentrating on education. In other words they imposed, as a therapeutic act, a rigid and severe scheme of education on the lines of the firmest Talmudic tradition. The guidelines of this preventive strategy (which looks somewhat like a defensive response to an accomplished fact) are made clear by an internal regulation laid down in 1714 by the Ashkenazi group, the *Capitoli della Fraterna Talmudh Torah della nazione degli ebrei tedeschi* (Chapters of the Talmud Torah Fraternity of the nation of German Jews). Their ideological assumptions and the ethical and religious view supporting them become clearer in a text published at the other end of the century, in 1782, by the most famous Venetian rabbi of the 18th century, Simone

Calimani: l'*Esame ad un giovane ebreo instruito nella sua religione* (Examination of a young Jew instructed in his Religion). The project was designed to revive the ideal of an integral Judaism, in the sense of a set of values on which to base all answers to the widest existential problems, and, as a plan for living, able to regulate every moment of daily life by the practice of the *mitzwoth* (precepts). At the same time it also sets out to offer the young Israelite a strong package of principles, Halakhic standards and holy writ to furnish him with a protective shield against outside attack. Beyond the rigid rules imposed inside the school, aimed at making the rabbis perfect models of Jewish life, the pages of the *Capitoli* place great emphasis on defining a complex and detailed plan of studies including, besides the "lay" subjects such as Italian and mathematics, the study of the *Torah* in the first cycle, the addition of prophetic passages and rabbinical comments in the second, access to the *Mishnah*, with the analysis of the prophets and hagiographers in the third, and access to the *Talmudh* in the fourth, complementing a course of training designed to make the pupil aware of his own spiritual identity and his personal Jewish integrity. Rabbi Calimani had been brought up on this model since the earliest years of his long life in the Ghetto and, after a life dedicated to study and teaching, he felt the need to take stock of his own Jewish condition and also consign a message to the younger generation by condensing the guiding principles of that all-round education in his *Esame*, making it a manual "aimed at the instruction of Israelite youth" and also consolidating the overall view that must sustain the pedagogic model to which every Jew should adhere. In the form of a dialogue between master and disciple, divided into ten sessions, he goes painstakingly through all the fundamentals of Hebrewism, defining them clearly and convincingly, and concentrating above all on the ethical aspect, which is nearest to his heart, because one cannot "give more opportune teaching to youth than that which treats of each person's duty towards God, to-

122

wards his neighbour and towards himself". The thoroughness of his exposition, his respect for the firmest orthodoxy as far as content is concerned, and his precision in tracing the spiritual itinerary of a true Jew, all combine to make the *Esame* the century's crowning example of ethical and pedagogic devotion. It is an exemplary work from many angles, but patently insufficient to cure symptoms of collapse which required quite a different type of support.

Simone Calimani, *Esame ad un giovane ebreo instruito nella sua religione* (1782), Tommasini, Gorizia 1783

the 1777 *condotta*, the hard economic reality clearly emerges from the taxation allotment: of 143 families registered for tax out of a total of slightly over 400, 113 were taxed between 1 and 149 ducats, 16 between 150 and 499, and 14 from 500 upwards. The manuscript in the Correr Museum, discussing the habit of the Jewish second-hand dealer, admits that "the Hebrew nation is never lazy" and undertakes "every kind of good exercise in various guise" providing an image of the Ghetto that, although dictated by prejudice, leaves no room for doubt, reporting the women as affected by eye trouble because of their ceaseless work of mending in poor light, and describing the terrible odour emanating from all the old material they were resewing, which even filled the narrow streets of the district.

There was also a significant fall in population, which dropped to 1717 souls altogether according to the 1790 census (Contento), perhaps made through the so-called "money harvest" — "Let every Head of Family rest advised to leave in his own house as many coins ... as there are individuals composing his own family" instructs a proclamation of 1795. Because of this, and the general circumstances, the revolutionary atmosphere, which led to the pulling down of the Ghetto gates, was once more powerless to produce substantial changes in the class relationships set up in this way. On the contrary, it could only endorse the differences between a minority with high economic standing and a majority bound to the instability of a modest subsistence, which was to characterize the social condition of the Jewish community in the 19th century. The disparity between family groups had replaced the imbalance between "nations" that had typified Ghetto life in the 16th and 17th centuries.

Analysis of surviving documents reveals that in the last years of the century the circumstances of a wide section of the Ghetto population were fairly precarious, depending on work that could not have ensured more than a very modest standard of living. It is true that a group of families, by virtue of their wealth, occupied positions of eminence in Venetian society, families such as Treves, Vivante, Gentili, Errera and Bonfil, who were holders of shipping licences, big ship-builders, textile manufacturers or great merchants. But it is also true that more than two thirds of Venetian Jews, mostly living in the Ghetto Nuovo, were still confined to rag-and-bone dealing or food retailing, or worked as servants or employees in poorly paid jobs. A form of census register, made by Sha 'ul Lewi Mortara in 1797 after the Ghetto gates were removed, offers quite an informative picture of the situation: of 1,600 inhabitants, the heads of families comprised 55 shopkeepers, 18 pawnbrokers, 75 rag-and-bone merchants, 24 brokers, 6 stockbrokers, 3 jewel brokers, 1 pearl broker, 1 bookseller, 1 cloth salesman, 1 furniture salesman, 4 haberdashers, 23 food retailers, 41 private agents, 8 tailors, 3 printers, 3 painters, 1 chair-mender, 1 engraver, 15 teachers, 21 priests, 5 doctors, 3 surgeons, 1 midwife, 5 porters, 2 hospice guardians, 3 postmen, 84 servants or cooks, 19 industrial workers, 29 beggars and 1 agriculturalist. But earlier, in 1779, after the conference called by the Senate to remedy the inopportune provisions of

123

Venice - Correr Civic Museum. G. Grevembroch, *Gli abiti de' veneziani* p.63, *A Jew*

The democratic government of the *Municipalità* (Municipality) which, with the French occupation (from 12 May to 17 October 1797), brought the principles of equality and fraternity to Venice, impinged unexpectedly on the stagnant reality of the Ghetto, but of course aroused enthusiasm and high hopes after centuries of unjust segregation; nothing, in fact, could have prepared people for such a radical change in the Jews' legal position as that provoked by the fall of *La Serenissima*. The provisional government issued a decree on 19 Messidor (7 July) in the name of liberty and equality, proclaiming that the "Jewish citizens" had equal rights, decreeing the election to the *Municipalità* itself of three deputies from them — Mosè Luzzatto, Isacco Grego and Vita Vivante were duly elected — and ordering, in its final paragraph, that the

124

Ghetto gates should be promptly removed, so that no separation should exist between the citizens of one and the same city. The inhabitants of the Jewish quarter, guided by their rabbis Emanuele Cracovia and Abramo Jona and the elected leaders, celebrated their regained freedom with hymns and public speeches in the Scola Spagnola on 21 Messidor (9 July), formulated the new problems arising within the community and began solid demonstrations of brotherhood by making collections for the poor in the nearest parishes. The solemn ceremony of beating down the gates, "symbols of anti-Jewish prejudice and hostility" was carried out on 22 Messidor (10 July). The *Gazzetta Veneta Urbana* reported the event on 12 July: "At 21 hours (about 3 pm), in the presence of many members of the civic guards corps and French soldiers in the main square of the Ghetto, with music and dancing by Jews with Christians, the gates were beaten down, splintered with axe-blows and burned amid public rejoicing for the fracture of these barriers of a barbarous prejudice". Jumping up onto the well in the square, "citizen" Raffaele Vivante read out a grandiloquent speech, which was later published: "We are now established in our natural rights, and the temple of honour, merit and virtue is no longer closed in our faces. That immense gap that separated us from other nations is

entirely removed, and lo here are overturned those formidable gates that kept our Nation confined as in a prison, and were reinforced by a thousand thousand iron bars invented by the most odious arrogance". He was followed by Abbot Starita then by Citizen Grego, who spoke in Venetian dialect, and the president of the *Società di Pubblica Istruzione* (Society for Public Education), Massa, made a speech at the Scola Spagnola. The day ended with a grand reception held in the evening at the Vivante house. The Ghetto itself changed its name and became the *Contrada dell'Unione*, as if wishing to wipe out, together with the name, centuries of underprivilege and discrimination. Yet all came to naught within the

brief span of a few months; the hopes and dreams were quickly dampened, the brief spell of liberty was soon only a memory. With the Treaty of Campoformio and the return of Austria, some of the old restrictions were resurrected and the Jews' situation returned to its former tensions and anxieties. Only the Ghetto gates were never replaced; they left, however, in the gateways leading to the district, the old marks of the bolts and the locks, still visible today like symbolic images, a perpetual reminder of the state of segregation that for three centuries dominated the Jewish community of Venice.

Venice - Ghetto Vecchio: The portico, looking towards Cannaregio

Graph of population development in
the Ghetto (1516-1797)

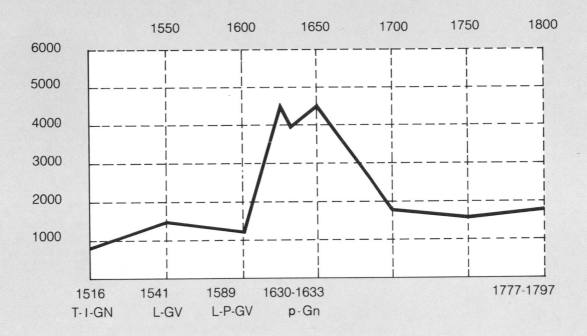

Key: T = Germans, I = Italians, GN =
Ghetto Nuovo, L = Levantines, P =
Ponentines (Sephardim), GV = Ghetto
Vecchio, p = Plague, Gn = Ghetto
Nuovissimo

It is extremely hard to establish the precise numerical strength of the three "nations" in the Ghetto during the centuries of their segregation, by reason of the absence of any reliable census and the shortage of surviving documents in community archives, also because of the ever-fluctuating numbers in the Levantine group, divided into "wayfarers" and "residents". On the basis, however, of estimates by Harris, who used suggestions by Beltrami, Contento, Beloch, Morpurgo, Luzzatto and Bachi, largely agreed today by Ravid, it is possible to draw a graph of the population development within the enclosure around San Girolamo that may at least approximate to its real size.

About seven hundred persons were confined in the Ghetto Nuovo in 1516, and they saw their numbers increase to about one and a half thousand between the thirties and 1541, when the Levantines were settled in the Ghetto Vecchio. By the end of the century, however, even with the arrival of the Ponentines

or Sephardim, their numbers had gone down to little more than a thousand, corresponding to about 1.2% of the entire Venetian population. The 17th century was the time of greatest development and consequently the greatest concentration in an increasingly crowded space. While it is impossible to credit the figure of 6,000 given by Simone Luzzatto in his *Discorso* (f.28 recto), it can be presumed from many indications that in the early decades of the century numbers rose to about 4,500, in other words 3.3% of the local population, while after the drop due to the disastrous plague of 1630 there was another increase, connected with the opening of the Ghetto Nuovissimo in 1633, reaching the earlier peak in the fifties, when many Ashkenazi refugees were coming in from Central Europe.

It can be seen that the population peaked at times when the "nations" were enjoying maximun stability, and inevitably dwindled as Venetian-Jewish society declined. Only in the second

half of the 17th century did the crisis begin that gradually thinned out the residents in the segregation quarter, making the Jews represent an ever smaller percentange of the total population of Venice. The emigrations due to the decline in commercial activity and the difficulties in the credit sector effectively reduced the population to about 1,600 souls in the first half of the 18th century, and this number was to decline further after the *condotta* of 1777, rise again slightly during the 1790s, and settle at a figure of 1,626 as given in an official register of 1797, the date when the Ghetto gates were removed. From then on, throughout the era of emancipation and right up to the Second World War, the Jewish group in Venice registered no remarkable variations.

Venice - Museum of Jewish Art: Silver-gilt prayer-book binding with symbolic motifs of a lion (strength, defence) and love (*"The love that the Lord shows towards you is as the love of a man for a woman"* — Tal. Bab., *Joma*, 54a)

BIBLIOGRAPHY

This list includes only particularly useful works in book form, and the more important essays and articles quoted in the text. Readers should turn to the usual sources for more exhaustive information.

AA.VV., *Gli Ebrei e Venezia — sec. XIV-XVIII*, Proceedings of the Convention held in Venice (Fond. Cini) on 5-10 June 1983, compiled by G. Cozzi, Ed. di Comunità, Milan 1987.

M. BENAYAHU, *Haskamah ureshuth bi-dhephusey Venezia*, M. ben Zevi - M. Rav Kook, Jerusalem 1971.

A. BERLINER, *Luḥoth 'abhanim. Hebräische Grabschriften in Italien. I. 200 Inschriften aus Venedig, 16 und 17 Jahrhundert*, Kauffmann, Frankfurt am Main 1881.

S. BERNSTEIN, *Luhoth 'abhanim. II. 180 Italian Hebrew Epitaphs of the Sixteenth - Nineteenth Centuries* in "Hebrew Union College Annual", X, 1935, pp. 483-552.

C. BOCCATO, *L'antico cimitero ebraico di S. Nicolò di Lido a Venezia* (Linograf Spa - Rome), Venice 1980.

R. CALIMANI, *Storia del ghetto di Venezia*, Rusconi, Milan 1985.

G. CARLETTO, *Il Ghetto veneziano nel '700 attraverso i catastici*, Carucci, Rome 1981.

D. CARPI, *The activity of the "Italian Synagogue" of Venice on behalf of the Jewish Communities of Eretz-Israel during the years 1576-1733*, Central Press (Jerusalem), Tel Aviv 1978.

D. CASSUTO, *Ricerche sulle cinque sinagoghe (scuole) di Venezia*, The Jerusalem Publ. House, Jerusalem 1978.

S. CIRIACONO, *Olio ed Ebrei nella Repubblica Veneta del Settecento*, Dep. Storia patria, Venice 1975.

U. FORTIS, *Ebrei e Sinagoghe*, Storti, Venice, new ed. 1984-1987.

U. FORTIS - P. ZOLLI, *La parlata giudeo-veneziana*, Carucci, Assisi/Rome 1979.

U. FORTIS (compiled by), *Venezia ebraica*, (with articles by Ashtor, Ioly Zorattini, Vanzan, Tamani, Grendler, Sereni and Zolli), Carucci, Rome 1982.

P.F. GRENDLER, *L'inquisizione romana e l'editoria a Venezia 1540-1605*, Il Veltro, Rome 1983.

A.C. HARRIS, *La demografia del Ghetto in Italia (1516-1797 circa)*, La Rassegna Mensile di Israel, Rome 1967.

D. JACOBY, *Les Juifs à Venise du XIVᵉ au milieu du XVIᵉ siècle*, in *Venezia centro di mediazione tra oriente e occidente (secoli XV-XVI) — Aspetti e problemi*, Olschki, Florence 1977, pp. 163-216.

P.C. IOLY ZORATTINI, *Gli ebrei a Venezia, Padova e Verona*, in *Storia della cultura veneta*, 3/I, Neri Pozza, Vicenza 1980, pp. 537-576.

P.C. IOLY ZORATTINI, *Gli ebrei nel Veneto dal secondo Cinquecento a tutto il Seicento*, in *Storia della cultura veneta*, 4/II, Neri Pozza, Vicenza 1984, pp. 281-312.

P.C. IOLY ZORATTINI, *Gli Ebrei nel Veneto durante il Settecento*, in *Storia della cultura veneta*, 5/II, Neri Pozza, Vicenza 1986, pp. 459-486.

P.C. IOLY ZORATTINI (compiled by), *Processi del S. Uffizio di Venezia contro Ebrei e giudaizzanti*, Olschki, Florence 1980-1985 (first four vols).

LEON MODENA, *Chayye' Yehuda*, edited by D. Carpi, The C. Rosenberg School, Tel Aviv 1985.

G.LUZZATTO, *Sulla condizione economica degli ebrei veneziani nel secolo XVIII*, in R.M.I. ("Scritti in onore di Riccardo Bachi"), XVI, 1950, pp. 161-172.

A.MILANO, *Storia degli Ebrei in Italia*, Einaudi, Turin 1963.

E. MORPURGO, *Inchiesta sui monumenti e documenti del Veneto interessanti la storia religiosa, civile e morale degli ebrei*, Del Bianco, Udine 1912.

R. MUELLER, *Les prêteurs juifs de Venise au Moyen Age*, in "Annales" XXX, 1975, pp. 1277-1302.

A. OTTOLENGHI, *Il Governo democratico di Venezia e l'abolizione del Ghetto*, in R.M.I., V, 1930, pp. 88-104.

A. OTTOLENGHI, *Per il IV centenario della Scuola Canton. Notizie storiche sui Templi veneziani di rito tedesco e su alcuni Templi privati con cenni della vita ebraica nei secoli XVI-XIX*, Tip. del Gazzettino illustrato, Venice 1932.

R. PACIFICI, *I regolamenti della Scuola Italiana a Venezia nel secolo XVII*, in R.M.I., V, 1930, pp. 392-402.

R. PACIFICI, *Le iscrizioni dell'antico cimitero ebraico a Venezia*, I, Palombo, Alexandria in Egypt 1937.

J. PINKERFELD, *Le sinagoghe d'Italia*, Goldberg's Press, Jerusalem 1954.

F. PISA, *Parnassim, le grandi famiglie ebraiche italiane dal secolo XI al XIX*, in "Annuario di Studi Ebraici (1980-84)" compiled by A. Toaff, Carucci, Rome 1984.

L. POLIAKOV, *I banchieri ebrei e la Santa Sede dal XIII al XVII sec*, Newton Compton, Rome 1974.

B. PULLAN, *La politica sociale della Repubblica di Venezia 1500-1620*, II, Il Veltro, Rome 1982.

B. PULLAN, *Gli ebrei d'Europa e l Inquisizione a Venezia dal 1550 al 1670*, Il Veltro, Rome 1985.

S.G. RADZIK, *Portobuffolè*, La Giuntina, Florence 1984.

B. RAVID, *Economics and Toleration in Seventeenth Century Venice*, Central Press, Jerusalem 1978.

B. RAVID, *The Establishment ot the Ghetto Vecchio of Venice, 1541*, in "Proceedings of the Sixth World Congress of Jewish Studies', II, Jerusalem 1975, pp. 153-167.

B. RAVID, *The first Charter of the Jewish Merchants of Venice, 1589* in A.J.S. Review, I, 1976, pp. 187-222.

B. RAVID, *The Jewish Mercantile Settlement of Twelfth and Thirteenth Century Venice: Reality or Conjecture?*, in A.J.S. Review,II, 1977, pp. 201-225.

B. RAVID, *The Socioeconomic Background of the Expulsion and Readmission of the Venetian Jews, 1571-1573*, in *Essays in Modern Jewish History*, Herzl Press, Rutherford-Madison-Teaneck 1982, pp. 27-55.

G. REINISCH SULLAM, *Il ghetto di Venezia. Le sinagoghe e il museo*, Carucci, Rome 1985.

G. REINISCH SULLAM, *Tesori d'arte ebraica a Venezia*, La Stamperia di Venezia, Venice undated.

C. ROTH, *Gli Ebrei in Venezia*, Cremonese, Rome 1933.

C. ROTH, *I Marrani a Venezia*, in R.M.I., VIII, 1933-34, pp. 232-239 and 304-314.

M.G. SANDRI - P. ALAZRAKI, *Arte e vita ebraica a Venezia 1516-1797*, Sansoni, Florence 1971.

G. SERMONETA, *Sull'origine della parola "ghetto"*, in "Studi sull'ebraismo italiano in memoria di Cecil Roth" Barulli, Rome 1974, pp. 185-201.

G. ZORDAN, *Le persone nella storia del diritto veneziano prestatutario*, Cedam, Padua 1973.

CONTENTS

128

א	'
ב	b
ב	bh
ג ג	gh g
ד ד	dh d
ה	h
ו	w
ז	z
ח	ḥ
ט	ṭ
י	y
כ	k
כ ך	kh
ל	l
מ ם	m
נ ן	n
ס	s
ע	'
פ	p
פ ף	ph
צ ץ	tz
ק	q
ר	r
ש	sh
שׂ	ś
ת ת	th t

Transliteration of Hebrew alphabet
To avoid over-complicated spelling, some simplification has been introduced.

I am grateful to Prof. Cesare Vivante for his kindness, and to my son Daniele for his help.

The publisher wishes to thank the libraries and archives which have contributed illustrations to this book.

Back cover. Perspective map of Venice by Giovanni Merlo, 1696

STORTI Edizioni srl
Tel. 041.5659057 / 041.5659058
Fax 041.5631157
Address:Casella Postale 361
30170 Mestre P.T. (VE)
Reprint: January 2000

www.stortiedizioni.it
e mail:edstort@tin.it